1970

WHAT DOES YOUR SOUL LOOK LIKE?

WHAT DOES YOUR SOUL LOOK LIKE?

EDITED BY GAIL NORTHE

PHILOSOPHICAL LIBRARY
New York

To

MINNIE AND HER SEVEN

"On the seashore of endless worlds children meet.
On the seashore of endless worlds is the great
meeting of children."
— Rabindranath Tagore

CONTENTS

PREFACE

". . . If you put a question to a person in a right way, he will
give a true answer of himself, yet he could not do this unless
there were knowledge and right reason in him already."
— *The Dialogues of Plato,* Benjamin Jowett,
4th Ed. Clarendon Press, Oxford, England, 1953.

"What does your soul look like?" This question was asked of
me in 1952. For the next seven years I asked the same question
of other adults and with less than a dozen thoughtful answers,
the usual reply was, "I haven't the slightest idea."

One day when I was talking with a little nine-year-old boy
who was blind, I said, "I have a very special question that
I believe you can answer. What does your soul look like?" In-
stantly, with a radiant smile on his face, he said, "It looks like
me!"

Such was the beginning of this book. To me, it is precious
and priceless because it is the hand-written record of the Journey
of the Human Soul as recorded by children and young persons
between the ages of five and nineteen years. It is honest, simple,
uninhibited, delightful, doubtful, troubled, seeking, sad, profound, timeless and universal. In it, racial origins, ages, colors,
religions, and different levels of educational, economic and
cultural backgrounds are all mixed together. As Plato, Plotinus,
Emerson, Tagore, Gandhi, Radhakrishnan and others tell us,
there is but one soul and each of us is a part of It — just as Cy,
age 12, says, "My soul is a tiny bit of the whole universe."

But Cy's answer and over two hundred answers from other
children and young persons raised many other questions: How,
with no prior discussion, could they spontaneously give such
answers, when they are 'only children'? Why the enormous range
in their replies — from "It looks like me but it's clear." (age
15) to ". . . You have to believe and understand yourself to say

11

why you act this certain way. . . Soul is love and hate; the difference between life and death." (age 10) Why was the vast majority of adults unable to give an answer? What has happened to us since we were young, when we may have given similar answers? To try to find out, I went to the hundreds of marginal notes and underlined sentences made during the years in some of my most beloved books. From these, selected passages from the writings of some of the world's greatest men throughout the ages were chosen to accompany the children's answers.

To the great and noble men who have been quoted, and to the children and young persons, we owe our deepest gratitude. From the children and young persons we get a newborn glimpse of faith, hope, love and wonder; of joy, beauty, wisdom and truth. From the philosophers, prophets, seers, we get the assurance, and again in our time, the admonition, that we can and must consciously and individually regain 'the lost unity' of our childhood if we are to find what our soul and Matt's soul 'is and wants'.

*　*　*　*　*

May I acknowledge my own personal debt: Often during the early hours between three and seven in the morning, while assembling the contents of this book, I felt an Inspiration and a Guidance far beyond my own meager capabilities. There were times when I knew that Someone Else was almost literally 'putting the pieces in the proper places' for me. I have no other credentials for having attempted to compile this book.

17 April 1969   Gail Northe

Reference Key and Acknowledgments

Excerpts from the books cited below appear throughout this volume. Rather than clutter up the pages with identifying footnotes, I have chosen to identify the source of each quotation by means of a letter symbol set in capitals immediately following the quotation. The full source information relative to each symbol is detailed below.

May I express my very grateful appreciation to the following authors, publishers, or copyright holders for granting permission to quote from the titles listed here.

AM   *All Men Are Brothers: Life and Thoughts of Mahatma Gandhi as Told in His Own Words,* Introduction by S. Radhakrishnan; Columbia University Press, New York, 1958.

CC   *Cosmic Consciousness: A Study in the Evolution of the Human Mind,* Edited by Dr. Richard Maurice Bucke; Innes & Sons, Philadelphia, 1901; E. P. Dutton & Company, New York, 1923.

CU   *The Cloud of Unknowing,* by An Unknown Author; Harper & Bros., New York, 1948.

DA   *Dictionary of American Maxims,* Edited by David Kin; Philosophical Library, Inc., New York, 1955.

ER   *Eastern Religions and Western Thought,* by S. Radhakrishnan; Clarendon Press, Oxford, England, 1939.

FL   *Founding the Life Divine,* by Morwenna Donnelly; Hawthorn Books, Inc., New York, 1958.

IV   *An Idealist View of Life,* by S. Radhakrishnan; George Allen & Unwin, Ltd., London, 1932.

N   *The Notebooks,* Vol. II, by Simone Weil; G. P. Putnam's Sons, New York, 1956.

P   *Papers From Eramos Yearbooks,* Edited by Joseph Campbell: "Spiritual Disciplines," by Heinrich Zimmer, page 14; Bollingen Series XXX, Copyright 1960 by The Bollingen Foundation, New York. Distributed by Princeton University Press, Princeton, N. J.

RA   *Radhakrishnan — An Anthology,* Edited by A. N. Marlow; George Allen & Unwin, Ltd., London, 1952.

RE   *Reincarnation — An East-West Anthology* and *Reincarnation in World Thought,* Compiled and Edited by Joseph Head and S. L. Cranston; The Julian Press, Inc., New York, 1961 and 1967 respectively.

SG   *Selections From Gandhi,* By Nirmal Kumar Bose; Navajivan Publishing House, Ahmedabad, India, 1948.

SM   *The Spirit of Man,* Edited by Whit Burnett; Hawthorn Books, Inc., New York, 1948.

SL   *Strength to Love,* by Martin Luther King, Jr.; Harper & Row, New York, 1963.

SR   *The Philosophy of Sarvepalli Radhakrishnan,* Edited by Paul Arthur Schilpp, Open Court Publishing Co., La Salle, Illinois, 1952.

T   *Tagore: A Biography of Rabindranath Tagore,* by Krishna Kripalani; Grove Press, Inc., New York, 1962.

TT   *A Tagore Testament,* by Indu Dutt; Philosophical Library, Inc., New York, 1954.

WG   *Waiting for God,* by Simone Weil; G. P. Putnam's Sons, New York, 1951.

WHAT DOES YOUR SOUL LOOK LIKE?

I

My soul looks like a
tiny bit of the whole
universe.

G Age 12

"I was set up from everlasting,
from the beginning, or ever the earth was.
When there were no depths, I was brought forth;
when there were no fountains abounding with water.
Before the mountains were settled,
before the hills was I brought forth:
While as yet he had not made the earth, or the fields,
nor the highest part of the world.
When he prepared the heavens, I was there:
when he set a compass upon the face of the depth:
When he established the clouds above:
when he strengthened the fountains of the deep:
When he gave to the sea his decree,
that the waters should not pass his command:
when he appointed the foundations of the earth:
Then I was by him, as one brought up with him:
and I was daily his delight, rejoicing always before him;
Rejoicing in the habitable part of his earth;
and my delights were with the sons of men.
(When the morning stars sang together,
and all the sons of God shouted for joy.)
Now therefore hearken unto me, O ye children:
for blessed are they that keep his ways.
Hear instruction, and be wise, and refuse it not . . .
For whoso findeth me findeth life,
and shall obtain favour of the Lord. . ."

> — Proverbs 8:23 through 31 (Job 38:7),
> Proverbs 8:32-33 and 35

"Was somebody asking to see the soul? See your own shape and countenance, persons, substances, beasts, the trees, the running rivers, the rocks and sands."

> — Walt Whitman (DA)

"When I consider thy heavens, the work of thy fingers, the moon and the stars which thou hast ordained; What is man, that thou art mindful of him? and the son of man, that thou visitest him?"

— Psalms 8:3-4

"I believe in absolute oneness of God and therefore also of humanity. What though we have many bodies? We have but one soul. The rays of the sun are many through refraction. But they have the same source."

— Gandhi (SG)

"Even in the earliest stage of his development. . .

"Lately I have been reading a book by Professor Caird in which he says, 'Though man is essentially selfconscious, he always is more than he thinks or knows; and his thinking and knowing are ruled by ideas of which he is at first unaware, but which, nevertheless, affect everything he says and does. Of these ideas we may, therefore, expect to find some indication even in the earliest stage of his development, but cannot expect that in that stage will appear in their proper form or be known for what they really are.' These ideas of which we are unconscious in the beginning, which yet influence us to say and do things, and prompt us into action and speech even in the earliest years of our immaturity without our knowledge, came to me as a revelation, which I tried to express in my small way in my short life-history. Whether it carried conviction or not is another matter, but there was no conceit. For this life-force is not anybody's exclusive property. . . . To acknowledge this life-force in one's life and in one's creation is not conceit. In fact, it is the opposite. For this life-force is not the property of any particular individual being; the whole world is motivated by it."

— Rabindranath Tagore (TT)

". . . this is his manhood."

"Every man possesses a special something which he calls 'his religion'. Yet, he does not know exactly what this means. He only knows that he is a Christian, a Mohammedan, a Vaishnava,

19

or that he is a pagan worshipper of the Deity of strength, etc., etc. And yet, though he is quite sure he belongs to this religion from the day he is born to the day he dies, it is in all probability not true. In the acceptance of a name, a barrier is so raised that the religion that is intrinsically his altogether escapes his notice. What is his religion? The religion that remaining unobtrusively in the depth of his mind is ever creating him. Men and animals are being moulded and are taking shape according to their deeply-implanted life-sense. Man possesses an extra awareness that is greater than his material sense — this is his manhood. It is this deep-abiding creative force which is his religion. So that in my language the word 'religion' has a profound meaning. The 'waterness' of water is essentially its 'religion', in the spark of the flame lies the religion of fire. Likewise, Man's religion is his innermost truth."

— Rabindranath Tagore (TT)

"And the Jews marvelled, saying, How knoweth this man learning, having never learned?

"Jesus answered them, and said, My doctrine is not mine, but his that sent me. If any man will do his will, he shall know of the doctrine, whether it be of God, or whether I speak of myself. He that speaketh of himself seeketh his own glory: but he that seeketh his glory that sent him, the same is true, and no unrighteousness is in him."   — John 7: 15-16-17-18

"There is nothing on earth that I would not give up for the sake of the country excepting, of course, two things and two only, namely, truth and non-violence. I would not sacrifice these two for all the world."   — Gandhi (SG)

"The end of life is not to be happy nor to achieve pleasure and avoid pain, but to do the will of God, come what may."

— Martin Luther King, Jr. (SL)

"He was not that Light, but was sent to bear witness of that Light. *That* was the true Light, which lighteth *every man* that cometh into the world."   — John 1: 8-9

20

II

THE JOURNEY OF THE HUMAN SOUL

MILESTONES

my Soul Looks Like aseed

_____

Billy McGovern.

Jan. 30th, 1966.   8,

"My soul is a seed
that must sprout and grow
and blossom."

— Debbie, age 12

"My soul is my conscience and my conscience is God in me."
— Chris, age 9

"I wanted to say something for what I thought my soul was really like and I suddenly got the thought that your soul (or flower) will open its petals (the bonds that tie us to mortal life) and if you let it, it will burst open to see the sun (God). And also other thoughts like: Let God live in you — He will help your soul to grow if you let Him. . . . This shows that every one is given the seed but whether nor not he or she is interested in it is whether they want to grow up."

— James, age 11

*   *   *

"Now the parable is this: The seed is the word of God."
— Luke 8:11

"And he said, so is the kingdom of God, as if a man should cast seed into the ground; And should sleep, and rise night and day, and the seed should spring and grow up, he knoweth not how. For the earth bringeth forth fruit of herself; first the blade, then the ear, after that the full corn in the ear."

— Mark 4:26-7-8

"For as the earth bringeth forth her bud, and as the garden causeth the things that are sown in it to spring forth; so the Lord God will cause righteousness and praise to spring forth before all the nations." — Isaiah 61:11

*   *   *

"My soul looks like joyness." — Mae Doris, age 12

"My soul looks like my soul." — Erika, age 10

"What does your soul look like? I think my soul is rounded out with love and care." — Cornelia, age 12

"It looks like a pretty butterfly with all kinds of colors. It is pretty because it is good." — Debbie, age 8

Karen   13.

1. My sole loves.

23

"What does your soul look like? A white horseshoe with yellow wings."   — Janet, age 11

"My soul looks happy and nice."   — Diane, age 10

"You can't see your soul but it is supposed to be a vision of goodness and loveliness."   — Gill, age 11

"It is a soul that loves people. Be kind to people."
                                    — John, age 10

"My soul is beautiful, it can have a meaning to it."
                                    — Patty, age 10

"My soul looks like my heart for it pounds like it, and that is where my love comes from. It has the color of beautiful red."
                                    — Debra, age 10

"About the size of your liver. Happiness and niceness might be in your soul — I don't really know but it might look like a pear. Full of the juices of life."   — Ellie, age 11

"My soul is a funny soul. It plays tricks on me. It is long and skinny. My soul has blue eyes and purple hair. I love my soul. Even though I never did see it."   — Bara, age 10

"My soul must be a beautiful thing because it is so nice and it helps me. I think it is a pretty little girl inside me. Whatever it is: *I love it*."   — Karen, age 10

"It looks like an angel."   — Roberto, age 13

24

"Hast thou heard the secret of God?". . . . . "I will pour out my spirit unto you, I will make known my words unto you."
— Job 15:8, Prov. 1:23

"Beloved, let us love one another: for love is of God; and every one that loveth is born of God, and knoweth God. He that loveth not knoweth not God; for God is love.
"No man hath seen God at any time. If we love one another, God dwelleth in us, and his love is perfected in us . . . and he that dwelleth in love dwelleth in God, and God in him. Herein is our love made perfect."
— John 4:7-8, 12, 16-17

"For in all of us are all things — at least as potentiality.
"Within us lies the predisposition to all things. . . The real fulfillment of such a stupendous play is the existence of God, not of the creature.
"Its reflection is found in the behavior of the child as long as it is little. . . In childhood the inner forces, which later are gradually inhibited and masked by social life and education and thrust back into the unconscious, are freely projected. They pour forth, naive and unrestrained."
— Heinrich Zimmer (P)

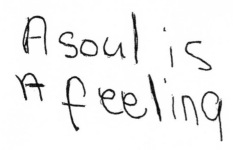

A soul is
A feeling

By Pamela

25

What Does Your Soul Look Like?

It looks like ME!
My soul looks like Myself.
My soul looks like the inside of myself.
It looks like — me.

I think my soul looks like me only it is clear white and invisible.
I think my soul looks like me but it is clear.
My soul looks like me, it is my ghost. It is like an invisible picture of me.
A soul is some feeling inside of you, and it is often used in expressions.
You can't see it, it lives inside you. My soul is invisible and when I die it will go to heaven to live.
My soul really I can't see. To me it is invisible. A soul is like a spirit as it says in the Bible.
I don't know what it looks like because you can't see it. You just know it is inside you.
My soul is invisible and I can think and feel.
Your soul does not look like anything — it is just a feeling.
A soul is a feeling. [The above answers, written together, were so beautiful they reminded me of some of the Psalms in the Bible. The following repeats each answer, individually, with the name of the child who wrote it.]

"It looks like ME!"   — Paul, age 9

"My soul looks like myself."   — Laverne, age 10

"My soul looks like the inside of myself."

—Sherian, age 12

"It looks like — me."   —Jim, age 12

"I think my soul looks like me only it is clear white and invisible."   — Susan, age 9

"I think my soul looks like me but it is clear."

— Regina, age 15

"My soul looks like me, it is my ghost. It is like an invisible picture of me."   — William, age 12

26

"You can't see it, it lives inside you. My soul is invisible and when I die it will go to heaven to live."

— Wanda, age 9

"My soul really I can't see. To me it is invisible, a soul is like a spirit as it says in the Bible." — Kim, age 11

"I don't know what it looks like because you can't see it, you just know it is inside you." — Jackie, age 7

"A soul is a feeling." — Pamela, age 15

Eva
age 13

My soul is invisable and I can not see, but I feel it all over me. My soul is very soft and tender with touch of pepper on one side.

"My soul is invisible and I can think and feel."

— Lucy, age 12

"Your soul does not look like anything — it is just a feeling."

— Cowandle, age 12

"It is short. It is thin. It has blue eyes. It is Jewish. It's me."

— Julie, age 10

"My soul looks like my heart. My soul is me."
— Amy, age 10

"My soul looks like me — Lori." — Lori, age 11

"I think my soul looks like me." — Maurice, age 10

"My soul looks like me. It is in the form of a human body clad in a green shirt and blue pants." — Danny, age 9

Steven 11

A regular boy with muscels.

"My soul looks like a girl's body — it is white brown and nice."
— Ada, age 11

"If your sole of your soul goes down, you buy another soul for your shoe. Ha-ha-ha-ha." — No name, age 9

"It's the shape of your body." — Gary, age 12

"My soul looks like part of my body." — Richard, age 8

"Our soul maybe looks sort of round and red, I think."
— Anita, age 12

"My soul looks like a girl with brown hair and eyes."
— Elisa, age 12

"I have blue eyes and blond hair." — Ellen, age 8

"I have brown eyes and dark brown hair."
— Jeremy, age 9

"My soul looks like the bottom of my shoe."
— Emily, age 8

"A lake of blood." — Jamie, age 8

28

"My soul looks like big and little red bones."

— Jeff, age 8

"My soul looks like air but lives in a shape of a person."

— Randy, age 11

"It looks like a ghost." — Mark, age 9

"The bottom of the shoe. What I think soul means — soul means the bottom of your shoe." — No name, age 9

"It looks like your ghost." — Elaine, age 12

"The bottom of a shoe or the inside of a person and his feelings."

— No name, age 9

"My soul looks like a brain." — Barbara, age 12

"What does your soul look like? It looks strong and healthy."

— Seth, age 9

"The sole is a fish.
It is a part of a shoe.
It operates the body of a man.
It is made up of 12 organs.
It is the body." — No name, age 9

Jaye   age: 10½

It has alot of bones it
also has alot of blood it
is all gushe inside I can
tell you for sure that
you would not want to
see it. It is a very un-
plesant thing to see.

29

"I don't know — it's round." — Brent, age 10

"I don't think soul looks like anything. It's just like air, we can't see it but we know it's there." — Anne, age 10

"I don't know." — Peter, age 11

"What does your soul look like? My soul does not look like anything. The soul is like a heart, brain, etc. The inner part of the body." — Stephanie, age 10

"My soul is an invisible object so I can't see it." —Marc, age 10

"My eyes are brown. My hair is brown-blond. I am Jewish." — Jill, age 11

"I think your soul looks just like a body that is very thin and ghost-like." — Fora, age 9

"My soul would look just like bones when I die." — Jeffrey, age 11

"My soul looks like a person." — Andrew, age 9

"My soul looks like a few free-form lines." — Susan, age 10

"A brain of a human body." — Paul, age 11

Daniel age 10

soul is all the same collor

"Your soul doesn't really look like anything because it doesn't have a color or shape."   — Natalie, age 11

"Your soul is your brain."   — Daniel, age 11

"I'm not sure."   — Laura, age 11

"It doesn't have any shape or color or form."
                          — Barbara, age 11

"Soul. Nobody knows, you can't see it."
                          — John, age 11

"My soul is the bottom of my shoe that makes me very happy."
                          — Jill, age 10

"My soul doesn't look like anything."
                          — Melodee, age 10

"What does your soul look like? It's light and dark, it's big and small, it's visible and invisible."   — Bruce, age 11

"I don't know, only God does."   — Alfred, age 10

"Your soul could be your heart."   — Scott, age 12

"A soul is part of your body."   — Susan, age 8

"Our soul I think looks like a ghostly figure that no one has ever seen, but I feel him sometimes when I think."
                          — Janet, age 10

"I think my soul looks like this — it has blue veins with a red liquid running through it. I have white bones and I have joints which have to do with my bones. My soul is me!"
                          — Ann, age 10

"My soul looks like a thing with blood, veins, and heart. My soul looks like me."   — Glenn, age 9

"My soul looks like myself except it is invisible so no one can see it which will never die."   — Martine, age 11

31

"My soul looks like a heart beating and pumping the blood. My soul is myself. It is the inside of me. My soul is the outside of me." — Scott, age 10

Q: What does My Soul look like?

A: *Like all the probelms and love in the world. And when do something bad there's probelms in your soul. When you do something good there's love in your soul.*

Dolly
age 11

"What is a soul? When you die some people think you turn into spirits and come down. The soul is inside your body. The soul cannot be seen. It only can be thought about. The soul is only a good thing to some people. Some kinds of religions believe that when you have been bad a lot you go to hell and the soul had been bad to you." — Courtney, age 9

"Your soul is part of your body that has feelings. It makes you feel bad if you did something wrong, it makes you feel good if you did something good. I don't think you can really see a soul." — Grace, age 9

"My soul looks like air to me but to a Certain Person it looks like myself." — Gregory, age 12

"The soul — a. No, you can't see the soul. b. Our soul can be our heart. c. Your conscience is your belief. A religious soul or conscience can be you believe in God or the devil or you can believe anything you want." — Indra, age 10

32

"It looks or it seems to me that it would be like an outline of your body none can see but God." — Dee Dee, age 11

"The soul cannot be seen. It can be in your heart or your mind. Your conscience is your belief. Your conscience is almost like your soul. Some people believe in good, some don't. Different people have different beliefs and different ideas."

— Monica, age 10

Gigi, Age 9

My soul is' a nice and bad. It looks like a something like other parts of my inside body Which is a nice soul. and ungley,

My soul looks like happiness in some ways and in some ways it looks like anger and in other ways it looks like sorrow for other people.

Angela
12

33

"My soul is good. But sometimes bad."   — Judy, age 10

"It is not any particular shape but the character and feeling of a person."   — Sharon, age 9

"My soul is the color of my heart and is my feeling.
My soul makes me nice and mean."   — Nancy, age 10

"Your soul does not look like anything — it is yourself and your feeling."   — Steven, age 11

"What does your soul look like? That is something I cannot tell because I don't know what it looks like. Although I can feel it — it feels like just me."   — Susan, age 11

"My soul looks like me but is see-through."
                          — Kim, age 10

"My soul is the way I act — it doesn't look like anything. If I act mean then my soul is mean. If I act nice, my soul will be nice."   — Josh, age 11

"Like heaven and hell — in a way of speaking."
                          — Paul, age 11

"You cannot see your soul — it doesn't look like anything. Your soul to me is your character or your personality."
                          — Diane, age 10

"It looks like a huge ball that tells your brain how you think and tells your brain that you did wrong or right. It also is the only thing that stays alive when your body is dead."
                          — No name, age 11

"My soul looks like (I really can't see it) an invisible thing. People keep saying after you die your soul goes to heaven. I sometimes guess it's true. I keep on thinking if I look real hard I will see one — that's silly though — I can't see — it kind of has moving things in it. Every time I think of it it looks a little different. It's shape is sort of like a person."
                          — Carol, age 10

Janet   Age 11

What does your soul look like?
Everybody's souls are different. Mine is the kind that makes me friendly and playful. Also my soul makes me what I am. When I'm mad my soul knows I am and it makes me show it. When I'm happy my soul knows it and it shows it. My soul has love in it for my parents and sisters and many dislikes. My soul has happiness, love, heat and many other things in it. I am happy with my soul and I hope it stays the way it is. Everbodys' souls contain love, hate, pain, Happiness, heat and cold.
    Like I said I like my soul and I want it to stay this way.

"My soul doesn't look like anything in particular. It looks like a little bit of good and a little bit of bad, something original and something from God."   — Kathy, age 11

"I think my soul is half full of gay colors and the other half filled with sad colors and the gay colors represent the good in life and the sad colors represent the sad."
                                                        — Liz, age 10

"I don't especially know what a soul looks like. I think it depends on who you are, what you look like, and if you are a good person you will have a good soul. I think it is a kind of spirit in a way and also I think it is a devil and an angel. I think I'm more an angel than a devil. I think it's 80% good and 20% bad."   — Aaron, age 9

35

Candy
12/7/67

What does your Soul look; like?

My soul is divided into parts.
Some of which are as complicated
as equations. It is my intermost
feelings, in which I share with
no mortal being.

The color of my soul varies
between brillant red to a shy
white. Its meaning to me is of
temendous value.

My soul is nothing more
nor nothing less than me. It
is filled with cigrette smoke, the
gaytee of children laughing,
the sound of muffled crying and
last but not least the smell of
freedoms.

I guess the things my
Soul is filled with most is
the memories of my parents
laughing.

8ᵗ ᵍʳᵈ.

36

"Maybe I think my soul, if I have one, looks like a city with a lot of buildings to go into. Many of them I haven't looked into yet. Many of them are good and bad. I'm my soul, I am the only one in it. I must pick one to go into. I'm not sure."

— Bill, age 13

"My soul is the invisible spirit which is the only everlasting part of my body. No human being can or could ever see my soul, but God can. What I mean is another spiritual being can. In God's eyes, my soul can either be clean from sin, or it may have sin and be dirty. It all depends on the things I've done. It does not look like anything or anybody. It is a spirit. It is the only part of myself that will, after I die, enter hell or heaven. My soul is invisible. It has no shape or form."

— Darlene, 11th grade

"The soul is an inner being or second you. Your soul is in the image of yourself, but is a transparent being. The soul is a spirit which involves you spiritually. To me it looks like a mass with wings that emerges from the body after death. If you've lived a life of evil doings, when it emerges from the body after death, it is black and has deep bloody scars. If you lived a life that is pure and in Christ, your soul is pure and white when it emerges from the body after death."

— Kathy, 11th grade

"My soul to myself is a spiritual thing inside me that no one or thing can see. My soul is the thing that acts for my character and for the things I do. It is also my mind and what type of moods I'll be in sometimes. My soul also gives me courage, energy and my vitality to do things and how my feelings are towards people I know. And my soul also influences me into things I do and say sometimes. That is my soul, I think."

— Sylvia, 11th grade

37

Cheryl
Dec. 7, 1967

*What does your
Soul look like?*

*My soul changes with the
day; changes with my mood. My
soul holds my feelings and
morals. It may express through
me good or bad. Although it's
not an object like your heart
in form, something material. It
works for you in many
ways. This may seem silly
that for something to do, which
is only spiritual.*

"The first thing I think of when I think of my soul is Jesus
Christ and Virgin Mary." — Yvonne, age 13

"My soul looks like a small castle in which God is the king and
Christ sitting on his side. My soul is like a very precious diamond
or ruby. My soul is my conscience that helps me iron out the
problems and troubles that I might have. It is also my person
who I can go to in silence and prayer to carry on. My soul also
helps me make decisions and gives me advice when needed. It
guides me in the path of righteousness and good doing — some-

38

times I go the opposite way and later say to myself — why? My soul brings me in close contact to God and his teachings."

— Leatha, age 17

"Star of David." — Seth, age 11

"Part of the human body that makes you feel and act spiritual."

— Cynthia, age 12

"Part of your body that still lives after you die. You can see your own soul or someone else's soul by what actions they take. Your conscience is what goes on in your mind. The soul is the same except that it goes on in minds and bodies."

— Miriam, age 10

Daniel 11½

It is dirty

Jean   age 8

I think my soul is a sin and looks so aful that I can't tell you

Rosann
11

It is like a black darkness inside of you.

39

"My soul is full of troubles . . . I am shut up, and I cannot come forth . . . Shall thy wonders be known in the dark? . . . Lord, why casteth thou off my soul? Why hidest thou thy face from me? I am afflicted and ready to die from my youth up: while I suffer thy terrors I am distressed."

— Psm. 88:3, 8, 12, 14-15

"The Lord is nigh unto them that are of a broken heart; and saveth such as be of a contrite spirit. Many are the afflictions of the righteous: but the Lord delivereth him out of them all." . . . "He shall deliver thee in six troubles: yea, in seven there shall no evil touch thee." . . . "Keep thy soul with all diligence; for out of it are the issues of life."

— Psm. 34:18-19, Job 5:19, Prov. 4:23

Lisa ⑩

What is your soul?
Your soul is sort of a shadow that is your figure after death. Sort of like your spirit.

What is your conscience?
A conscience is like an inner voice which tells you what is right and wrong. It really doesn't do any good because it always makes you feel you've done something bad after you've done it or else when your in the middle of it.

THE END

40

"Why art thou cast down, O my soul? and why art thou disquieted within me?" — Psm. 42:11

"That the soul be without knowledge, it is not good. . . . The foolishness of many perverteth his way: and his heart fretteth against the Lord. . . . In your patience possess ye your soul . . . For godly sorrow worketh repentance. . . ."
— Prov. 19:2-3, Luke 21:19, II Cor. 7:10

"Who knoweth not in all these that the hand of the Lord hath wrought this? In whose hand is the soul of every living thing, and the breath of all mankind." . . . "Know ye not that ye are the temple of God, and that the Spirit of God dwelleth in you?"
— Job 12:9-10, I Cor. 3:16

"Thy way and thy doings have procured these things unto thee; this is thy wickedness, because it is bitter, because it reacheth unto thine heart." . . . "But every one shall die for his own iniquity." . . . "For every man shall bear his own burden." . . . "(God) will render to every man according to his deeds: . . . of the Jew first, and also of the Gentile. . . . For there is no respect of persons with God." . . . "Even a child is known by his doings, whether his work be pure, and whether it be right."
— Jer. 4:18, Jer. 31:30, Gal. 6:5,
Rom. 2:6, 9 and 11, Prov. 20:11

"The preparations of the heart in man, and the answer of the tongue, is from the Lord. All the ways of a man are clean in his own eyes; but the Lord weigheth the spirits." . . . "There are many devices in a man's heart; nevertheless the counsel of the Lord, that shall stand." . . . "The law of his God is in his heart."
— Prov. 16:1-2, Prov. 19:21, Psm. 37:31

"My son, despise not the chastening of the Lord; neither be weary of his correction: For whom the Lord loveth he correcteth; even as a father the son in whom he delighteth."
— Prov. 3:11-12

41

"Thou Lord, which knoweth the hearts of all men. . . ."
"The Spirit itself beareth witness with our spirit, that we are
children of God: And if children, then heirs; heirs of God, and
joint-heirs with Christ: if so be that we suffer with him. . . ."
. . . "God is our refuge and strength, a very present help in
trouble. Therefore will not we fear, though the earth be removed,
and though the mountains be carried into the midst of the
sea. . . . Be still, and know that I am God."
"Then are they glad because they be quiet; so he bringeth them
unto their desired haven. Oh that men would praise the Lord
for his goodness, and for his wonderful works to the children
of men! . . . Whoso is wise, and will observe these things, even
they shall understand the lovingkindness of the Lord."
                    — Acts 1:24, Rom. 8:16-17,
              Psm. 46:1-2 and 10, Psm. 107:30-31 and 43

"All life is eternal, there is none other; and all unrest is but the
struggle of the soul to reassure herself of her inborn immortality."
                              — Bronson Alcott (RE)

"Our own spiritual ascents and falls, and those of the beings
we love, have to do with the other world, but they are also
events that take place here below, in time. On that account
they are details in the immense sea of events and are tossed
about with the ocean in a way conforming to the will of God."
                              — Simone Weil (WG)

"The golden rule of conduct . . . is mutual toleration, seeing
that we will never think alike and we shall see Truth in fragments
and from different angles of vision. Conscience is not the same
thing for all. Whilst, therefore, it is a good guide for the individual conduct, imposition of that conduct upon all will be
an insufferable interference with everybody's freedom of conscience."   — Gandhi

"There are some who assume that when we see what is right
we will do it. It is not so. Even when we know what is right

it does not follow that we will choose and do right. We are overborne by powerful impulses and do wrong and betray the light in us. 'In our present state we are, according to Hindu doctrine, only partly human; the lower part of us is still animal; only the conquest of our lower instincts by love can slay the animal in us.' "

— Dr. S. Radhakrishnan (AM)

"For ye are yet carnal: for whereas there is among you envying, and strife, and divisions, are ye not carnal, and walk as men?" . . . "For we know that the law is spiritual: but I am carnal. . . ." "For when the Gentiles, which have not the law, do by nature not; but what I hate, that do I." . . . "This I say then, Walk in the Spirit, and ye shall not fulfill the lust of the flesh. For the flesh lusteth against the Spirit, and the Spirit against the flesh: and these are contrary the one to the other: so that ye cannot do the things that ye would."

— I Cor. 3:3, Rom. 7:14-15, Gal. 5:16-17

"Therefore thou art inexcusable, O man, whosoever thou art that judgest: for wherein thou judgest another, thou condemnest thyself; for thou that judges doest the same thing. . . . And thinkest thou this, O man, that judgest them which do such things, and doest the same, that thou shalt escape the judgment of God? . . . For not the hearers of the law are just before God, but the doers of the law shall be justified.

"For when the Gentiles, which have not the law, do by nature the things contained in the law, these, having not the law, are a law unto themselves: which show the work of the law written in their hearts, their conscience, also bearing witness. . . . For he is not a Jew, which is one outwardly. . . . But he is a Jew, which is one inwardly . . . in the spirit and not in the letter; whose praise is not of men, but of God."

— Rom. 2:1, 3, 13-15 and 28-29

"For this commandment which I command thee this day, it is not hidden from thee, neither is it far off. It is not in heaven,

43

that thou shouldest say, Who shall go up for us to heaven, and bring it unto us, that we may hear it, and do it? Neither is it beyond the sea, that thou shouldest say, Who shall go over the sea for us, and bring it unto us, that we may hear it and do it? But the word is nigh unto thee, in thy mouth, and in thy heart, that thou mayest do it. See, I have set before thee this day life and good, and death and evil. . . ."

— Deut. 30:11-15

Chand   *age 9*

I don't belive in this junk but this is what I think it looks like

I think it looks like the cuculore stum

"I don't believe I have a soul — can't think of anything else to say so I'll just write some lines. (a full page of lines) The end."   — Rich, age 13

"I think it is stupid."   — No name, age 10

"A stupid question — it is the body."   — No name, age 10

"I think my soul is not a very religious type. It is more atheistic in the way I react to thoughtful or religious questions, etc."   — Paul, age 13

"The mind — the thought. LSD STP POT COCOA LEVE"
— No name, age 10

"When you die you are buried in a grave and you are not alive anymore."   — Rebecca, age 11

*   *   *

"Many there be which say of my soul, There is no help for him in God." . . . "What is the Almighty, that we should serve Him? and what profit should we have, if we pray unto Him?" . . . "If we have forgotten the name of our God, or stretched out our hands to a strange god; shall not God search this out? For He knoweth the secrets of the heart."
— Psm. 3:2, Job 21:31, Psm. 44:20-21

". . . and they say, Who seeth us? and who knoweth us?" "And thou sayest, How doth God know?"
— Isa. 29:15, Job 22:13

"Therefore shall they eat of the fruit of their own way, and be filled with their own devices." . . . "And He gave them their request; but sent leanness into their soul."
— Prov. 1:31, Psm. 106:15

"Ye shall seek me, and shall not find me: and where I am, thither ye cannot come." . . . "They shall go with their flocks and with their herds to seek the Lord; but they shall not find Him; He hath withdrawn Himself from them." . . . "and when He hideth *His* face, who then can behold Him? whether it be done against a nation, or against a man only. . . ."
— John 7.34, Hosea 5:6, Job 34:29

"Because I have called, and ye refused; I have stretched out my hand, and no man regarded; but ye have set at nought all my counsel. . . . Then shall they call upon me, but I will not answer; they shall seek me early, but they shall not find me: For that they hated knowledge, and did not choose the fear of the Lord." . . . "For what is the hope of the hypocrite, though he hath gained, when God taketh away his soul?"
— Proverbs 1:24-25 and 28-29, Job 27:8

"And I will say to my soul, Soul thou hast much goods laid up for many years; take thine ease, eat, drink and be merry. But God said unto him, Thou fool, this night thy soul shall be required of thee; then whose shall those things be which thou hast provided? So is he that layeth up treasure for himself, and is not rich toward God." . . . "For what is a man profited if he shall gain the whole world, and lose his own soul?" . . . "They that trust in their wealth, and boast themselves in the multitude of their riches; none of them can by any means redeem his brother, nor give to God a ransom for him: For the redemption of their soul is precious. . . ."

— Luke 12:19-21, Matt. 16:26, Psm. 49:6-8

"Hear this, all ye people; give ear, all ye inhabitants of the world: Both low and high, rich and poor, together. My mouth shall speak of wisdom." . . . "It shall even be as when a hungry man dreameth, and, behold, he eateth; but he awaketh, and his soul is empty. . . . Forasmuch as this people draw near me with their mouth, and with their lips do honour me, but have removed their heart far from me, and their fear toward me is taught by the precept of men: Therefore, behold . . . for the wisdom of their wise men shall perish, and the understanding of their prudent men shall be hid. . . . They also that erred in spirit shall come to understanding, and they that murmured shall learn doctrine."

— Psm. 49:1-3, Isa. 29:8, 13, 14 and 24

"I have come to the fundamental conclusion that if you want something really important to be done, you must not merely satisfy reason, you must move the heart also. The appeal of reason is more to the head, but the penetration of the heart comes from suffering. It opens up the inner understanding in man." — Gandhi (SG)

"It is easy enough to say, 'I do not believe in God.' For God permits all things to be said of Him with impunity. He looks at our acts. And any breach of His law carries with it, not its vindic-

46

tive, but its purifying, compelling punishment. God is the hardest taskmaster I have known on earth, and He tries you through and through. And when you find that your faith is failing or your body is failing you, and you are sinking, He comes to your assistance somehow or other and proves to you that you must not lose your faith and that He is always at your beck and call, but on His terms, not your terms."

— Gandhi (SG)

"God is that indefinable something which we all feel but which we do not know. To me God is Truth and Love, God is ethics and morality. God is fearlessness, God is the source of light and life and yet He is above and beyond all these. God is conscience. He is even the atheism of the atheist. He transcends speech and reason. He is a personal God to those who need His touch. He is purest essence. He simply Is to those who have faith. He is long suffering. He is patient but He is also terrible. He is the greatest democrat the world knows. He is the greatest tyrant ever known. We are *not,* He alone Is."

— Gandhi (SG)

*　　*　　*

"I cannot tell what my soul looks like because it is not a thing of materialistic value. It is something that is invisible but yet it can be felt. It is something that is not found in any medical book or encyclopedia but it is something that is given us by God Himself to those who accept Him."

— Clarence, age 17

"My soul looks like an object every day when God watches over us and tells us what is right."　　　— Diane, age 13

"My soul is very small in terms of the world, but very large within me."　　　— Marcia, age 13

*　　*　　*

"Behold, all souls are mine; as the soul of the father, so also the soul of the son is mine."　　　— Ezekiel 18:4

47

I believe that the soul is a part of one's mind based on faith in a universal force which enables them to do incredible works according to the strength of this faith.

Bruce
age 14

[Conversation with three young brothers. Ed.]

Q. What does *your* soul look like?
A. My soul looks like a spirit.   — Curt, age 10
Q. Do you have a soul, too?
A. If one guy has one, everybody has one.
                                          — Darrow, age 7
Q. What is God?
A. He's Spirit, too.   — Mark, age 8
Q. Do you think people can talk with God?
A. Sure. Anybody can.   — Mark

"I think my soul is part of my heart — not physically. I think
if you had enough trust in Him you could do anything you

48

desire — for instance, turn the world upside down in two seconds. My soul is your heart." — Dicky, age 10

* * *

"Then said I, Ah, Lord God, behold, I cannot speak: for I am a child. But the Lord said unto me, Say not, I am a child: for thou shalt go to all that I shall send thee, and whatsoever I command thee thou shalt speak. Be not afraid of their faces: for I am with thee. . . ." — Jeremiah 1:6-7-8

"Jesus said unto him, If thou canst believe, all things are possible to him that believeth." . . . "For verily I say unto you, That whosoever shall say unto this mountain, Be thou removed, and be thou cast into the sea; and shall not doubt in his heart, but shall believe that those things which he saith shall come to pass; he shall have whatsoever he saith." . . . "If ye have faith . . . nothing shall be impossible unto you." — Mark 9:23, Mark 11:23, Matt. 17:20

"Prayer is the very soul and essence of religion, and therefore, prayer must be the very core of the life of man, for no man can live without religion. . . . Prayer is not asking. It is a longing of the soul. It is daily admission of one's weakness. It is better in prayer to have a heart without words than words without a heart." — Gandhi (SG)

"In all thy ways acknowledge Him, and He will direct thy paths." . . . "The Lord is at hand. Be careful of nothing; but in every thing by prayer and supplication with thanksgiving let your requests be made known unto God. And the peace of God, which passeth all understanding, shall keep your hearts and minds. . . ." — Prov. 3:6, Phil. 4:5-6-7

"God is the sole object of prayer. Prayer is movement toward God." — Simone Weil (N)

"Our Father which art in heaven. . . ." — Matt. 6:9

"The Our Father contains all possible petitions; we cannot

49

conceive of any prayer not already mentioned in it. It is to prayer what Christ is to humanity. It is impossible to say it once through, giving fullest possible attention to each word, without a change, infinitesimal perhaps but real, taking place in the soul. . . . " 'Our Father which art in heaven.' He is our Father. There is nothing real in us which does not come from him.

"We belong to him. He loves us since he loves himself and we are his. . . .

" 'Hallowed be thy Name.' . . . Man has access to this name, although it also is transcendent. It shines in the beauty and order of the world and it shines in the interior light of the human soul." — Simone Weil (WG)

My soul looks like a force with direction.

Preston age 19

Monique Age 10

My Soul looks like bones with some meaning. I don't know what that meaning is but I'd like to find out. My soul inside I think makes me do the ~~things~~ things I do.

"My soul is like a source of energy that you really can't see."
— Ruth, age 10

"It is the mind of the person that controls what the body does. My soul is me. People see me as I act. That is what my 'soul' looks like." — Fred, age 13

"My soul looks like a semi-circle. Some of my soul is higher than the bottom part — some is equal to the bottom."
— Pamela, age 10

"I don't know. I've never met it. I don't know what it looks like. I don't think you can see it. A soul is just a way of describing yourself, not physically, but what kind of person you are inside. Your body is just a housing for your soul."
— Greg, age 14

"My soul is the spiritual part of me and it tells me how I feel toward other people. Your soul is what you are — not what you know." — Imogene, age 17

"What does my soul look like? It is that part which God controls. It is that most precious part which cannot be destroyed by man. But you can't see it 'cause it is a spirit and that can only be described by God. But it guides us through the path of righteousness if we only yield to it."
— Geraldine, age 17

* * *

"Strange is our situation here on earth. Each of us comes for a short visit, not knowing why, yet sometimes seeming to divine a purpose." — Albert Einstein (DA)

"The end of life is not to be happy nor to achieve pleasure and avoid pain, but to do the will of God, come what may."
— Martin Luther King, Jr. (SL)

"Then saith he unto them, My soul is exceeding sorrowful, even unto death: tarry ye here, and watch with me. And he went a

51

little farther, and fell on his face, and prayed, saying, O my Father, if it be possible, let this cup pass from me: nevertheless not as I will, but as thou wilt." — Matt. 26:38-39

"For thine is the kingdom, and the power, and the glory for ever. Amen.
"For if ye forgive men their trespasses, your heavenly Father will also forgive you. . . ." — Matt. 6:13-14

"And he said, a certain man had two sons: And the younger of them said to his father, Father, give me the portion of goods that falleth to me. And he divided unto them his living.
"And not many days after the younger son gathered all together, and took his journey into a far country, and there wasted his substance with riotous living. And when he had spent all, there arose a mighty famine in that land; and he began to be in want. And he went and joined himself to a citizen of that country; and he sent him into his fields to feed swine. And he would fain have filled his belly with the husks that the swine did eat: and no man gave unto him.
"And when he came to himself, he said, How many hired servants of my father's have bread enough and to spare, and I perish with hunger! I will arise and go to my father, and will say unto him, Father, I have sinned against heaven, and before thee, And am no more worthy to be called thy son: make me as one of thy hired servants. And he arose, and came to his father. But when he was a great way off, his father saw him, and had compassion, and ran, and fell on his neck, and kissed him.
"And the son said unto him, Father, I have sinned against heaven and in thy sight, and am no more worthy to be called thy son.
"But the father said . . . let us eat and be merry: For this my son was dead, and is alive again; he was lost, and is found. And they began to be merry." — Luke 15:11-22, 23-24

"When the soul returns to its true home, there is always joy."
— Martin Luther King, Jr. (SL)

"Verily, verily I say unto thee, Except a man be born again, he cannot see the kingdom of God." — John 3:3

"To recover the lost unity is to be reborn.
"Spiritual life is not to be confused with the instinctive or the unconscious. It is true that religious teachers tell us that we cannot enter the kingdom of heaven unless we become little children . . . the unconscious unity of life which made instinctive knowledge possible is sundered by the rise of intellect which helps us to know ourselves and control the forces of nature. Since the primaeval unity is broken, man is uncertain and wavering. We seem to be alienated from nature, leading sceptical, artificial and self-centered lives. If intellect is to be brought closer to life, it must combine with instinctive knowledge. Such a combination is what we possess in intuition. It has the directness and unity of instinctive knowledge as well as the consciousness of the intellectual. It is not confused irrationalism or irresponsible mysticism.
"When the prophets refer to the virgin outlook of a child, they have in view the second innocence which comes after knowledge and not the first which precedes it. The spontaneity of the child is not a substitute for insight. The spirit which is the unconscious beginning must become the conscious ending of our life. Children enjoy an innocence, a sincerity, an integrity, born of harmony between themselves and their lives. They live in peace; they tell no lies; they do no wrong. They surrender themselves to spontaneity. Their behavior is a perfect expression of their being. Our intellectual consciousness has driven us out of that wholeness of being. To regain that integrity, to attain to a life where knowledge and being are not divorced from each other is the essence of human evolution. To recover the lost unity is to be reborn. It is the secret of spiritual life, the mystery of the kingdom of God." — S. Radhakrishnan (IV)

"At the same time came the disciples unto Jesus, saying, Who is the greatest in the kingdom of heaven? And Jesus called a little child unto him, and set him in the midst of them, And

53

said, Verily I say unto you, Except ye be converted (change), and become as little children, ye shall not enter into the kingdom of heaven. Whosoever therefore shall humble himself as this little child, the same is the greatest in the kingdom of heaven."

— Matt. 18:1-2-3-4

"If a man die, shall he live again? all the days of my appointed time will I wait, till my change come."

— Job 14:14

> 3/ question:
> WhaT does your Soul
> look like?
> It Looks Like A
> Railroad track
> that never ends
>
> Barby   10
> (2 name)   age

"Is there a heaven?"
"I think that you kind of come back until you're perfect, and then, well, there isn't a place, but I think you go to God when you're perfect." [This is what one young person replied in answer to the question. According to the London *Daily Telegram* for June 8, 1960, there is a strong preoccupation today among senior school children with some form of reincarnation, judged by informal talks among them on religious education by a research group under Leukes of Oxford University Education Department.] (RE)

"People who think deep are kin even though they aren't relations."   — Debbie, age 12

Jessica (11)

"Your soul is your inner thought of mind or being. There is no inner location of it really, it is just you. It is your good or bad, strong or weak, perfect or imperfect. It is your thoughts above such things as reincarnation.

"What is a soul — a conscience is something like a voice inside you that tells you right or wrong. The soul is your body or yourself. Maybe after death your soul will turn into dust or you may be cremated which means to get burned. Reincarnation is what some religions think. For instance, they think if you were good in your before life, you might be something good in your next life. In other words, life always goes on. If you were bad in your before life, you would be an animal or a bird or anything but a human."   — Erica, age 10

[Following are extracts from *The Record of A School* by Elizabeth Peabody, a book that contains her eye-witness reports of actual classes conducted by Bronson Alcott at Temple School in Boston in 1835. The class was discussing Wordsworth's *Ode to Immortality*.]

January 30. . . .

"What do you mean by birthday?"
"Birthday is the day of which the spirit is put into the body," said one boy.
"Did you get that idea in this school?" said Mr. Alcott.
"I never thought of such subjects before I came to this school," he said.

55

One of the boys added that he had always had an indistinct idea that the soul lived before the body, that there was a transmigration of souls. . .

February 4. . .

Some expressed the idea that the soul shaped and made the body; others that the body was made, and the soul put into it. "Which is right," said one boy.
"That is more than I can tell you, but I incline to the first opinion. You are all nearly right, however; you have important ideas; birth is not the beginning of the spirit; life is the remembrance, or waking up of the spirit. All the life of knowledge is the waking up of what is already within." (R.E)

"Our life is a step on a road, the direction and goal of which are lost in the infinite. On this road, death is never an end or an obstacle, but at most the beginning of new steps. The development of the soul is a continuous process, though it is broken into stages by the recurring baptism of death."
— S. Radhakrishnan (RA)

"The goal ever recedes from us. The greater the progress the greater the recognition of our unworthiness. Satisfaction lies in the effort, not the attainment. Full effort is full victory."
— Gandhi (SG)

"God is acceptance." . . . "Death is the meaning of life."
— Cheslovich Mackaiev

"In your patience possess ye your souls." . . .
". . . Count it all joy when ye fall into divers temptations; knowing this, that the trying of your faith worketh patience. But let patience have her perfect work, that ye may be perfect and entire, wanting nothing." . . . "Be ye therefore perfect, even as your Father which is in heaven is perfect."
— Luke 21:19; James 1:3-4; Matt. 5:48

"And as Jesus passed by, he saw a man which was blind from his birth. And his disciples asked him, saying, Master, who did sin, this man, or his parents, that he was born blind? Jesus answered, neither hath this man sinned, nor his parents; but that the works of God should be made manifest in him."

— John 9:1-2-3

"And this is life eternal, that they might know thee the only true God. . . .

"I have glorified thee on the earth: I have finished the work which thou gavest me to do. And now, O Father, glorify thou me with thine own self with the glory which I had with thee before the world was."   — John 17:3-4-5

"I was set up from everlasting, from the beginning, or ever the earth was."   — Proverbs 8:23

III

[Note: One day, in August 1963, I was sitting by the frog pond with my young friend, Billy, then age five. During our conversation, I said, Billy, could you tell me something about God. When I heard what he said, I ran in the house and got my old 2A Brownie camera and asked him to tell me again. This is what happened. . .]

"God is in. . . Frog. . ."

"God is in. . . Bird. . ."

"God is in — the grass. . ."

"God is in — THE WHOLE WORLD. . ."

"And — God is in my heart."

[The next day Billy went on a picnic. As he was walking along the river bank with his mother, he said,

> "God made the rocks
> God made the river
> — but who made God?"

This is Billy, who at age eight years, said, "My soul looks like a seed."]

"In whose hand is the soul of every living thing, and the breath of all mankind."   — Job 12:10

IV

DRAWINGS

I believe
in signs and symbols
I believe
in God.
God gives us
signs and symbols
for our
undeveloped
souls.

[Note: Some of the following drawings, which were made by the children as their 'answers' to the question: "What Does Your Soul Look Like?", were sent to England to the eminent British poet and art critic, Sir Herbert Read, in September 1968. He was asked if he would kindly make a comment about them that might be included in this book. The following reply was received from his son, Mr. Benedict Read:

"Stonegrave, York, England   30.ix.68

Thank you for your letter of September 19th.
I am very sorry to have to inform you that Sir Herbert Read died on June 12th last. . . . Perhaps when your book is published you might like to send us a copy so that it may join the other material collected by Sir Herbert on the subject of Children's Art."

Pertinent to this book, you will enjoy reading the articles by Sir Herbert Read and Dr. Paul Dudley White in the *What I Have Learned*, A Collection of 20 Autobiographical Essays by Great Contemporaries from the *Saturday Review*, published by Simon & Schuster, 1968. Also, in the book *Spiritual Disciplines* (see acknowledgements) the chapters by C. G. Jung and by M. C. Cammerloher may add significant meaning to these "simple" children's drawings as would the book, *The Soul of The Universe* by Gustaf Stromberg, David McKay Company, Philadelphia, 1940.]

what i think is a soul
By Peter
It is yellow and white and round.

Andrea 7½

Deborah   age 8½

I think my sole
is myself. So I
drew myself looked
the way I looked
like today
Sunday, October 20 th

Its red and
its inside me.

Eve.

MAGGIE'S answer

— what is a soul —

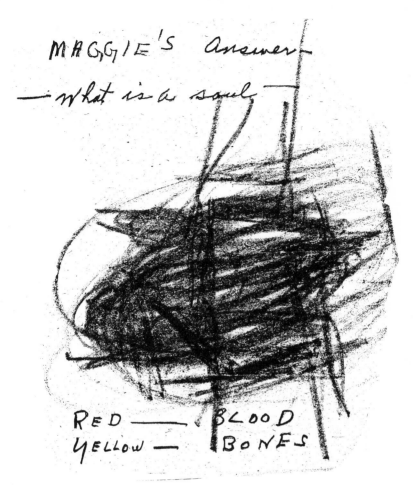

RED ——— BLOOD
YELLOW — BONES

What does your soul look like?

(?) — age 11

My soul looks just like me, except that
its invisible. Deep down inside me my soul is good,
even though I don't always show it outside. My
soul is not always good and its not always bad.
scale of soul:

Bad 600's

67

Richard 7

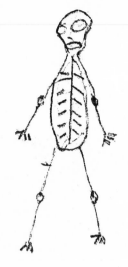

Monster

Larry 8

A bar of Boap

What Does My Soul Look Like   Kathy Age 11

I think my soul looks like
two people in one. One a
big red devil and the other a
little white angel. The devil
is an ugly big red thing and the
angel is a very dainty little
girl.

Spira

My soul looks like any other
soul probly at lease thats what
I feel. It's probly rather jelly-
like, And hope-fully good
and kind. It's pt also
probly funny shaped as
this.

70

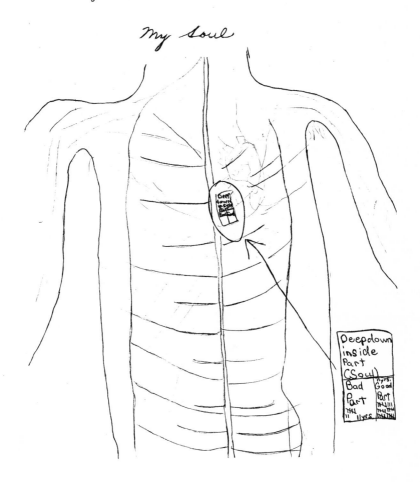

My Soul   Beth
                                            11

    My Soul is part of a shew

---

② My soul is _love_. Your
soul is _Peace_. My
soul is part of my
Shew. But most of all
my soul is me myself
and I.

My soul is the good
of me.
My soul is the bad of
me.

72

Bad

Good

WAlTer 8

and half *bad* ~~my soul~~ is half good

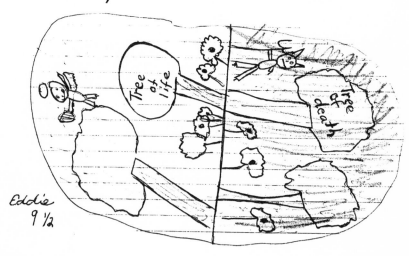

Tree of life

Tree of death

Eddie
9 ½

MARVEL AGE 9

a soul looks like a

Denise 9½

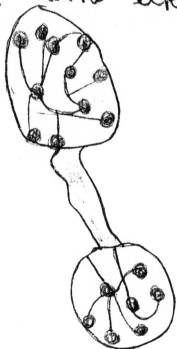

74

What does your soul look like?

I think your soul looks like a
maze of lines. These lines
represent your emotions and feeling,

life and death, and your body functions,
sorrow and ~~Happiness~~, Heat and cold, and
pain.

75

Another example is: "It is so that life can be changed into worship, by putting behind it the spirit of transcendent and universal love, the seeking of oneness, the sense of oneness; by making each act a symbol and expression of Godward emotion or a relation with the divine; by turning all we do into an act of worship, an act of the soul's communion, the mind's understanding, the life's obedience, the heart's surrender." — (Synthesis of Yoga) 51

At this point I was so filled with pure love, truth and happiness, I came to the highest point of cosmic consciousness I ever have had. During the summer I had two blooms, as I told you, however, they were not as big as this one. Then my thoughts started rolling. I wanted to say something of what I thought my soul would really like and I suddenly got the the thought that your soul (or a flower) will open its its pedals (the bands that tie us to mortal life) and burst open to see the sun (God).
Also other sorts thoughts like:
Let God live in you, he will help your soul grow if you let him and those which I won't go into.

(See letter from James, p. 113, dated
October 23, 1963)

Mary - 10

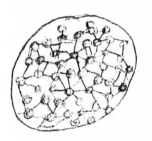

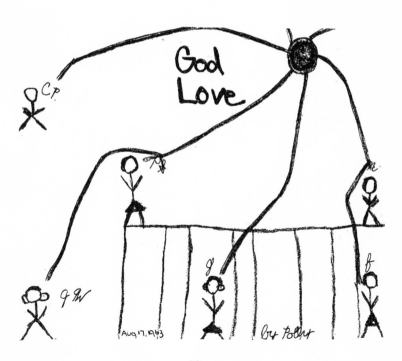

God
Love

Aug 17, 1963

77

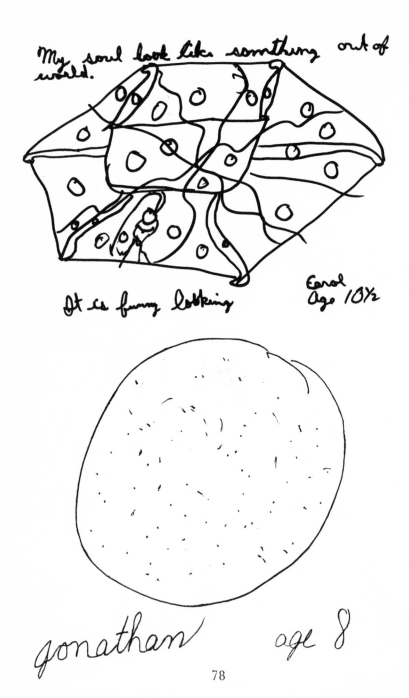

My soul look like something out of world.

It is funny looking

Carol
Age 10½

jonathan   age 8

ART HAS SOUL

"All true art is thus the expression of the soul. The outer forms have value only in so far as they are the expression of the inner spirit of man. . . . All true art must help the soul to realize its inner self." — Gandhi (SG)

V

THE VOICE IS THE SOUND OF THE SOUL

"One of the dreams of my life had been a contribution to science to establish a hazarded theory, namely, that the most essential differentiations of the soul of man from the soul of the brute will find their ultimate roots in articulate speech — that, in short, the human soul is speech . . . the origin of language and the relation of speech to the human soul must in any case concern soul-life . . . language must assuredly play an important part in the manifestation of soul qualities."
— Charles Granville, *The Westminster Review* (1910)

"Dr. Peter Ladefoged, head of UCLA's Phonetics Laboratory, . . . using a device called a sound spectrograph which draws 'visible speech' patterns on paper, is able to look at basic characteristics of speech. . . He points out that speech includes such information as the speaker's age, sex, emotional state and those characteristics that help to identify him as an individual. With the spectrograph Dr. Ladefoged and his colleagues are working to identify the acoustic signals that enable a hearer to know the speaker and his mood . . . acoustic signals that correspond to emotional moods. Dr. Ladefoged reports that 'condescending speech often has a wider pitch range, and anger is conveyed by a narrower pitch range and shorter voiced periods. . . .' "
— from a University of California Clip Sheet, January 10, 1967

"He that hateth is known with his lips, and layeth up deceit within him; when he speaketh fair, maketh his voice gracious, believe him not."   — Prov. 26:24-5

"There are murmurers, complainers . . . and their mouth speaketh great smelling words." . . . "They think that they shall be heard for their much talking."

— Jude 16; Matt. 6:7

"The words of his mouth are smoother than butter, but war was in his heart: his words were softer than oil, yet were they drawn swords." . . . "And truth is fallen in the streets." . . . "A good man out of the good treasure of the heart bringeth forth good things: and an evil man out of the evil treasure bringeth forth evil things."

— Psm. 55:21; Isa. 59:14; Matt. 12:35

"Whoso keepeth his mouth and his tongue keepeth his soul from trouble." — Proverbs 21:23

Michael 11½

It's like a glob that makes me feel good and sometimes sad and it looks like a big gigantic glob with a real big MOUTH!!!

"There are, it may be, so many kinds of voices in the world, and none of them is without signification. Therefore if I know not the meaning of the voice, I shall be unto him that speaketh a barbarian, and he that speaketh shall be a barbarian unto me. . . . Yet in the church I had rather speak five words with my understanding, that *by my voice* I might teach others also, than ten thousand words in an unknown tongue."

— 1 Cor. 14:10-11 and 19

"If now thou hast understanding, hear this: Hearken to the voice of my words." — Job 34:16

"The hearing ear and the seeing eye, the Lord hath made even both of them." — Proverbs 2:6

"The human voice is the organ of the soul."

        — Longfellow (DA)

"My harp also is turned to mourning, and my organ into the voice of them that weep."
"Thou hast turned for me my mourning into dancing . . . to the end that my glory, my tongue, my soul, may sing praise to thee."
"The voice of joy and the voice of gladness, the voice of the bridegroom and the voice of the bride and the voice of them that shall say, Praise the Lord . . . for the Lord is good; and his mercy endureth forever."

        — Job 30:31; Psm. 30:11-12; Jer. 33:11

"The Lord hath given me the tongue of the learned, that I should know how to speak a word in season to him that is weary: he wakeneth morning by morning, he wakeneth mine ear to hear as the learned."   — Isa. 50:4

"And the Lord said unto him, Who hath made man's mouth? or who maketh the dumb, or deaf, or the seeing, or the blind? have not I the Lord? Now therefore go, and I will be thy mouth, and teach thee what thou shalt say."

        — Exodus 4:11-12

"And all bear him witness, and wondered at the gracious words which proceeded out of his mouth." . . . "And they were astonished at his doctrine: for his word was with power." . . . "For he taught them as one having authority and not as the scribes."   — Luke 4:22, 32; Matt. 7:29

"Every one that is of the truth heareth my voice."

        — John 18:37

"A mysterious law makes it so that a human being who touches God is, at that moment, beautiful to look upon. So likewise are the lines, sounds, combinations of words, etc. that issue from him in that state."   — Simone Weil (N)

VI

"IF ANYTHING IN THE PAST IS WORTH PRESERVING,
SURELY IT IS THE HISTORY OF THE SOUL."*

"As the very atoms of the earth and the stars of the sky seek harmony with the system which binds them to a cosmic unity, so the souls of men seek harmony with the spirit which makes them one." — John Haynes Holmes (DA)

"God looked down from heaven upon the children of men, to see if there were *any* that did understand, that did seek God."
— Psalms 53:2

* G.E. Woodberry (DA)

85

CHRIS

Age 9 through 18

[Note: Chris is our eighteen-year-old nephew. He lives in a mid-western state, and although he has been to visit us only three times, we carry on a sort of unwritten correspondence, and continue it in letters when we feel like it. Chris' mother died when he was six years old, in 1956. He spent Christmas with us that year, with his father and older brother, Peter. In 1959, Chris came for a month's visit in August.

One day he suggested that we do "something special" for his mother. After discussing many ideas, we decided to build a little rock church, on the rock wall, under the cherry tree. As we were fitting the rocks in the front left-hand corner, I told Chris that people often put messages in cornerstones, and if he would like to write one, we could put it in an aspirin bottle, and his note would become "the cornerstone." He went in the house and was back in a few minutes. "Here," he said, "you read it." It said:

"We are building this little church for my mother who died when I was six. I am now nine and I hope when I get to be a man I will feel as I do today. Chris"

— Cornerstone date: Aug. 7, 1959

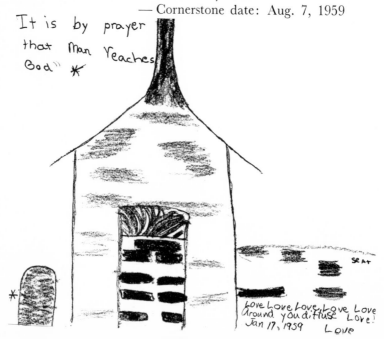

It is by prayer that Man reaches God" *

Love Love Love, Love Love
Around you diffuse Love!
Jan 17, 1959   Love

[Note: This is the sketch for the church drawn by Chris when he was 9. The words below had been put there the January before. . . . And this is what it became. . . .]

[The following letters from Chris are self-explanatory.]

"My soul is my conscience and my conscience is God in me."
— Chris, age 9

[Note: Chris forgot that he told me this, which I had written down. When I asked him last year if he would answer the question: "What does your soul look like?", he wrote me the following letter.]

17 April 1968

"Dear Gail:

"I've thought and thought about your question but I am finding it more and more difficult to answer — the more thinking I do. The soul of a person is the complete being. It's made up of his personality, conscience, subconscience, emotions, co-ordination, and is a transcendent of God. It can only be seen by God and I think that is the way He looks at us — as complete, complex, total beings influenced — whether we admit to God or not — by God.

"The soul isn't a visible thing because it contains too many human qualities. The soul is the whole being that God sees us for and that's why He can overlook some of the bad and stupid things we do because He can see the good at the same time. Since the soul is the complex man it contains the divine, and this is how God reaches us — through the soul.

"However, we know that the soul — or the complete being — is not released from its physical bonds until the body dies and the soul passes into another realm or dimension — I will not elaborate on what realm or dimension because that is a discussion for debate in itself — Another reason I feel we can't see the soul is because we never see the whole person. . . WE NEVER SEE OURSELVES TOTALLY AS GOD SEES US so we can't see our soul.

"If I was going to place the soul somewhere in the body — even though I don't feel it is an organ, or even has a central receiving center — IT IS JUST THERE AS WE ARE — There are many reasons and we don't know them all. But if I had to place it somewhere in the body I would put it in the center of the heart because when the body dies, the soul is released so why couldn't the heart release the soul when it stopped. But that is just a thought — a possible solution for people who have to find the soul in the body in order to understand it. Well, I hate to say it, Gail, but in effect I am telling you that my mind cannot visualize a soul — I don't think it looks like an upside bowl or something.

"I think the soul is the complete being and I think God is the only one that can see the complete being — because that is how He sees us and that is what the soul has got to be — the complete personality without the hangups of a body which we need on earth but we can leave behind at death because it won't be necessary in the next realm — I don't believe.

Love,

Chris"

June 21, 1968

"Dear Gail,

"As to your question: What Does Your Soul look like? — all

the answers were from persons in my graduating class. However, not all my class turned in their answers. There were 198 students in all, there are 47 answers here.

"I changed the wording of your question because since the general opinion was that the soul is not visible and students felt this way — that the wording might make them think or visualize something that they had taken for granted as a non-tangible thing. Anyway, I think the response, the answers were more serious and contained a greater degree of thought. In my questionnaire — which I typed myself and the teacher dittoed for me — I asked these questions: 1. How would you define the soul? 2. What do you think it looks like, or don't you think it's visible? — explain. 3. Do you think there is a relationship between God and the soul? And I listed all the denominations and asked which one they agreed with most. I thought their religious preference might be important to you because you can often tell who has been indoctrinated and who hasn't.

"I didn't have to get special permission through the Superintendent of Schools because our Senior Class was initiating The Modular System of Flexible Scheduling into LHS — next year LHS is going all 'MOD', all grades and subjects. In this system students can lecture to their whole class so I was able to give out this questionnaire as a Quest Project and required no special permission or red tape.

"Well, Hope I helped.

Love,

Chris"

[Note: In the following answers from the members of Chris' High School Graduating Class of 1968, their names and their religious preferences have been omitted. No theme or order in the arrangement of their answers has been attempted.]

> "The soul is that part of us which governs all that we do — Our conscience, thoughts, beliefs, dreams, and actions are all motivated by our soul. It is not visible it is a spirit. Yes, I have been taught to believe — there is a relationship between God and the soul."

How would you define the soul? ... *The soul is not physical but is the state a soul is in but it is a mass of energy and since energy and mass are interchangable that is why it is possible to an existence after death.*

What do you think it looks like, or don't you think its visible, (explain) *It is not visible, like energy, but its effects are noticable, you can feel it.*

Do you think there is a relationship between God and the soul? *I find the being of a God very difficult to comprehend but I believe in an existence after this world.*

Indicate the denomination you agree with most.
Roman Catholic
United Methodist
Lutheran
Baptist
Evangelical
Jehovah Witness
Mission Covenant
Seventh-Day Adventist
Christian Scientist
Assemblies of God
Jewish
Other   *I believe in self religion*

"You can't define it — this is the most ridiculous question I have ever heard of. There is no definite definition of the word — soul."

> "Really your soul is your conscience and nothing more — the way you react to right and wrong. Are your thoughts visible to you when you think of them — no, so neither is your soul. Actually, according to the Bible God made everything — if God made man, then He made man with a conscience for right and wrong."

"An inner feeling which is indefinable. It isn't anything you can see; the soul is in us and is what God uses in our hearts to come to us."

> "A little bowl inside of you. God is the soul."

"The soul is the mind — a small part of the brain. It occupies no space but it governs us during our lives. It is also conscience. It is not visible but it controls our thinking and it can be trained through ideas of others. The only relation that God has with our soul is that He can save it. The person thinks for himself and he can save his soul if he wants to."

"It is something you agree that we all have and need in order to exist. Right now God owns our soul and when I die my soul goes to heaven."

"I think the soul is an emotion box which is what causes us to love, hate, or care for someone — it is given to each one to choose. It exists as a feeling forever. God created the souls of all human beings — people who believe in Him go to heaven to live with Him — in the form of a soul."

How would you define the soul? *that is man by which he reveals himself as alive, as an individual, and as a thinking, willing and knowing being - man's spiritual and intellectual nature.*

What do you think it looks like, or don't you think its visible. (explain) *it is not physically visible, rather it becomes obvious through one's character + actions.*

Do you think there is a relationship between God and the soul? *I definitely think so mainly because of my faith*

"The soul is a person's inner conscience. It is invisible. I think the soul is a part of God."

"A dream made up by a race which needed something to explain its existence. Their vanity in not believing that the world ceases existence at death created it. The soul does not exist. The story of God needed a way of associating directly with man's needs."

92

"That part of you that makes you an individual: personality, temper and all those things that set you apart from all other people. The soul cannot be seen, smelled or tasted, but its presence can be sensed by some supersensitive people. I don't know what I think quite for sure — about the soul's relationship to God — but my guess would be no."

"Soul to me is a person's inner feelings or conscience that makes up the soul. Soul can vary from person to person. It can have an appearance through a person's personality and actions. God created man and by man's soul God has a way to communicate with man."

"Your soul is your inner being. It controls you, and it belongs to God. It is something God put there."

"It is the inner meaning of a person — the basis of life. Spirit."

"I really have no definition for the soul except that it is the part of our bodies that lives on after we are dead. We Christians seem to believe there is a relationship between God and the soul."

"Non-believer."

How would you define the soul? *the mind*

What do you think it looks like, or don't you think its visible. (explain) *You can't pick out your soul like you can an appendix, It can't be seen*

Do you think there is a relationship between God and the soul? *there is no god*

"I believe that the soul is the part of the body that is most associated with God."

"Soul is our mind and conscience. It makes us like God since it is a spirit. It is what makes us human since it is our free will, conscience, etc. It's not really visible but you can tell something as to its condition by the way a person acts and looks (neat, eyes shine, etc.) to some extent. The soul is what gives man his likeness to God."

"As the spiritual part of a human, the most inner and basic root of a person. No, I don't think it's visible. A person who doesn't believe in God wouldn't believe that he'd have a soul — there would be nothing for the soul to exist for."

"Something imaginary symbolized as conscience. When we don't have sins our soul is dear — if we have sins our soul is dirty and black."

"I think the soul is a feeling we have for God — I believe it is because of God that we even have a soul."

"It is a way of life and God knows by this — and your conscience."

"Your inner self — a spiritual mark which you obtain from God after baptism. Your soul goes to heaven, not your body — and your sins are marked on your soul and carried with you. It is not visible but scientists have said that with ultra violet light they have seen the soul rising from the dead. No definite shape."

"To me the soul is a feeling without our body — it is a feeling of faith — a feeling of love for God and wanting to do what is right — to be a Christian, live a quiet and peaceful life in the eyes of God."

"I think the soul is a feeling of love for God. The soul is a feeling of guilt if you do something against God."

How would you define the soul? The soul is the driving life force that enables one to move. One could still be alive and if he had no soul he would be like a vegetable.

What do you think it looks like, or don't you think its visible. (explain) The soul is invisible. Since the soul is the life force it could be located in the brain since brains have been kept alive without a body.

Do you think there is a relationship between God and the soul? Yes because the soul is what sustains life. Man has been able to make life (the DNA molecule) but he could never make a complete brain. So some kind of Super Being must have.

"It is the inner part of you. It is invisible. It can't be seen — it is just there."

"The soul is an inner being found in man that distinguishes him from lesser animals. During our life I believe the soul is not visible but rather a feeling in you. In the after life I believe it is visible, probably because I am unable to conceive of life different from ours. The soul was given to us by God for the purpose of an after life."

"Your soul is the deep feeling you have toward something — good or bad. It may feel something evil and yet in action you do something good. It is your conscience — you are built around your soul. Your soul goes to heaven and your body remains on earth and turns to ashes."

"The soul is an inner part of a person's body which has no feeling. A person just knows it is there because

95

of his religion. Religions are based on saving your soul
so that when you die, it will go to heaven."

"A soul is a place within you — there are your
sins or extra grace from God. You always think of
your soul as white and every time you sin there is a
black mark on it. I sometimes think it is your conscience. You can ask God's forgiveness for your sins
and your soul is cleansed — you receive extra grace
from God which also helps."

"Each person has one. God has His way of taking us
home — we are not to know everything. It isn't visible
— it is just a term that God judges you by. There
would be no use to live if you weren't rewarded for the
life you have lived on earth, because He has promised
a home for us who believe on his name — this is what
He judges us on."

"The soul is what makes you do the things you do.
I think God is the ruler over your soul — and looking at it that way you could say God is your soul."

How would you define the soul? *The soul is a metaphysical
thing which is composed of energy. It is the
spark of life and is animate.*

What do you think it looks like, or don't you think its visible,
(explain) *It isn't visible because it is energy.
However, its effects can be seen.*

Do you think there is a relationship between God and the soul?
*Yes, but it is a relationship in which God
controls the soul. The soul is completely subordinated
to God.*

96

"The soul is our being. It is not a thing we can grasp. It is our feelings; our subconscious mind behind our known mind. It is the make-up in a person that makes him what he is. It is there but it is not available to us. Its relationship to God we can't alter."

"The soul is God and God is the soul."

"An imaginary feeling that carries all your feelings, faith and sins when you die. It is a feeling or spirit — it is your eternal life."

"Soul is a person's form of life after death. He has a soul if he goes to heaven or hell. A person believes in a soul only if he believes in a religion."

"I think the soul is something that is just us — it is a feeling you have for God."

"That part that goes to heaven after the body dies."

How would you define the soul? A. soul is something that exists inside of you. I or consciences would come in the same category as the soul. I believe that the Holy Spirit speaks to you through here. The soul is you after death.

What do you think it looks like, or don't you think its visible. (explain). No don't think that a soul is visible. After death it may be visible but no one knows for sure.

Do you think there is a relationship between God and the soul? Yes, I think that God created the soul and He uses it. It could be our soul that starts us on our search for a greater being and so we find God.

"The soul is a state of mind that does not actually exist until after death. I believe that it is the good

97

part of the human brain. It isn't visible; it doesn't appear until after death and then it doesn't exist on earth. God made the soul — the relationship is that of the creator to that which is created."

"The part of the being that God is most concerned with — it indicates what the person really is. It is not a physical part of the anatomy — the soul is what God really sees."

"I believe that the soul was made in creation and has lived all the time since creation, and it will live forever if you get everlasting life on the judgment day. Soul is not your physical being that can be turned back into dust, but it lives until you are doomed to hell. I think that God made us children of God and He has shown it in many ways."

* * *

"Study of other religions besides one's own will give a grasp of *the rock bottom unity of all religions* and afford a glimpse also of the universal and absolute truth which lies beyond the 'dust of creeds and faiths'." — Gandhi

". . . thy brother . . . or thy son, or thy daughter, or the wife of thy bosom, or thy friend . . . *is* as thine own soul." — Deuteronomy 13:6

"What the Scriptures say, whether they are true or not, I do not know. . . The religion we get acquainted with from outside, from books of Scriptures, can in no way become our own religion. Its association with us is only a matter of habit. To unfold one's religion within oneself is the life-long aspiration of every human soul. It has its birth in acute suffering." — Rabindranath Tagore (TT)

Oct 3, '68

DEAREST AUNT GAIL,

FIRST I MUST APOLOGIZE FOR NOT WRITING
SOONER BUT TO BE VERY HONEST (AND WE
SHOULD BE!) I WAS TOO POOR TO EVEN
BUY STAMPS. I DON'T WANT THIS TO SOUND
LIKE A PLEA FOR MONEY. IT'S NOT. I JUST
WANTED YOU TO KNOW WHY I HADN'T WRITTEN.
THIS SCHOOL IS VERY EXPENSIVE AND IT'S VERY
HARD ON DAD - AND I DON'T WANT MY EDUCA-
TION TO BE A HAND OUT. I HAVE BEEN WORKING
AT THE LEAMINGTON HOTEL 3-5 hrs a nite
as A POSTER OF EVENTS 7 DAYS A WEEK FOR
THE LAST THREE WEEKS. I JUST HAVEN'T BEEN
PAID YET - WON'T BE UNTIL THE 15th SO
THINGS HAVE BEEN VERY TIGHT. BUT I'LL
VERY WELL SURVIVE. MONEY ISN'T EVERYTHING
AND I'D RATHER BE SHORT OF IT THAN HAVE
TOO MUCH. I APPRECIATE THINGS I DON'T
HAVE MUCH MORE. WHEN I GOT YOUR
CHECK (THANKS SO MUCH BY THE WAY)
I WENT TO SEE RUTH AND HAD - AS
ALWAYS A MARVELOUS TIME. THANK-YOU
I'VE BEEN WORKING SINCE. ALSO THANKS
FOR THE CLIPPING. ONE OF THE KIDS
SAW IT AND WANTED TO KNOW WHO IT
WAS. I TOLD THEM HE WAS MY UNCLE
AND AS USUAL THEY DIDN'T
BELIEVE ME. THEY THEY decided I MUST
BE VERY RICH. I TOLD THEM I WASN'T
BUT EVEN IF I WAS IT WOULDN'T MAKE
ANY DIFFERENCE JUST AS I BELIEVE

IT DOESN'T TO C.R. HE IS CAUTIOUS ABOUT
IT EVEN IF HE DOESN'T HAVE TO BE.
THAT IT WHAT I HAVE LEARNED. — TO
BE CAUTIOUS ABOUT IT ~~ALL~~ SINCE WE
OBVIOUSLY ARE TOLD AND FIND IT IS
NECESSARY ALTHOUGH NOT ESSENTIAL.
EVERY DAY OF MY LIFE IS MORE IMPORT-
ANT THAN MAKING A MILLION TO ME.
JUST LIVING IN GOD'S WORLD AND BEING
AWARE AND ALIVE. ALTHOUGH SOMEDAY
I'D LIKE TO BE RICH I KNOW THAT
IF I DIDN'T LIKE BEING RICH ID GIVE
IT ALL AWAY, I MET A FELLOW WHO
INHERITED 4 MILLION DOLLARS WHEN
HE WAS 21. HE DID THE THINGS
HE WANTED (TRAVEL) FOR A YEAR
THEN BUILT A MILLION DOLLAR ~~HOUSE~~ AND
GAVE IT TO A FRIEND. THEN HE BOUGHT
MERCEDES BENZES FOR THE PEOPLE WHO
HAD PICKED HIM UP WHEN HE HAD HITCH-
HIKED. BROKE, HE HITCHHIKED TO LOS ANGELES
TO RESUME SCULPTING AND RECENTLY
RETURNED TO WISC. ON A VISIT. HE IS NOW
VERY SUCCESSFUL. I WISH PETE HAD LEARN-
ED ABOUT MONEY — BUT IVE LEARNED
FROM HIS MISTAKES TOO.
    I MOVED FROM THE AWFUL RESIDENCE
HALL INTO THE UPSTAIRS OF A VERY OLD RESTORED
HOUSE. IT IS LOVELY AND I AM VERY
HAPPY HERE. ITS A BEAUTIFULLY REDONE
HOME. I LIVE WITH 4 OTHER GUYS WHO ARE
VERY NICE AND VERY CIVILIZED. THE DORM WASN'T!

I ALSO MET A GIRL WHO HAS THE "SENSE
OF MIRACLES" I STARTED TO TALK TO HER
ABOUT HOW I COULD TALK TO GOD INFORMALLY
ANYTIME AND HE KNEW WHAT I WAS DOING
OR WHAT I WANTED. HE LISTENED AND HELPED
ME OUT - ALWAYS. MAYBE NOT IN THE WAY
I ASKED OR WHEN BUT ALWAYS SOMEHOW.
ALL I DO IS ASK - AND THANK HIM WHEN HE
HELPS. HE'S ALWAY THERE BUT I DON'T HAVE
TO PREACH ON STREET CORNERS OR SUCH —
SHE KNEW EXACTLY WHAT I MEANT - SHE
HAS THE SAME SENSE. SHE SAID SHE HAD
NEVER TALKED TO ANYONE WHO COULD
UNDERSTAND WHAT SHE WAS MEANT -
WHY SHE COULD BE CLOSE TO GOD WITH-
OUT READING THE BIBLE EVERY DAY OR
GOING TO CHURCH EVERY SUNDAY. BUT
SHE KNEW I UNDERSTOOD AND I KNEW
SHE DID. I'VE ALWAYS BEEN TOO FAR ABOVE
THE LEVEL OF WHO I WAS TALKING TO
ABOUT THAT EXCEPT FOR YOU. I DON'T
MEAN BETTER THAN THEM - IT'S JUST THAT
EVERYTHING I SAY GOES OVER THEIR
HEAD THEY CAN'T GRASP IT!
  WELL WE WERE ON THE SAME LEVEL.
IT WAS ALMOST LIKE TALKING TO YOU
AGAIN / AND YOU TELLING ME ABOUT
THE ANTS ON THE PORCH.
WELL I JUST WANTED YOU TO KNOW
HOW I WAS AND TELL YOU WHAT WAS
GOING ON BECAUSE I KNOW YOU ARE
ALWAYS INTERESTED. I LOVE YOU.
                              Chris

"Give us this day our daily bread. . ."   — Matt. 6:11

" 'Give us this day our daily bread' — the bread which is supernatural. . . There is a transcendent energy whose source is in heaven, and this flows into us as soon as we wish for it. It is real energy; it performs actions through the agency of our souls and of our bodies.
"We should ask for this food. At the moment of asking, and by the very fact that we ask for it, we know that God will give it to us. . . We cannot store it."   — Simone Weil (WG)

"Immortality will come to such as are fit for it; and he who would be a great soul in the future must be a great soul now."
                — Ralph Waldo Emerson (DA)

"And every man shall receive his own reward according to his labour. For we are labourers together with God . . . ye are God's building." . . . "Partakers of the divine nature." . . . "The Lord *is* with you, while ye be with him; and if ye seek him, he will be found of you; but if ye forsake him, he will forsake you." . . . "The spirit of man *is* the candle of the Lord."
                — I Cor. 3:8-9; II Pet. 1:4
                II Chron. 15:2; Prov. 20:27

"Incline your ear, and come unto me: hear, and your soul shall live. . . ." . . . "Then shalt thou call and the Lord shall answer; thou shalt cry, and he shall say, Here I *am*. . . .
"And if thou draw out thy soul to the hungry, and satisfy the afflicted soul; then shall thy light rise in obscurity, and thy darkness be as the noon day: And the Lord shall guide thee continually, and satisfy thy soul in drought . . . and thou shalt be like a watered garden, and like a spring of water whose waters fail not. And they that shall be of thee shall build the old waste places: thou shalt raise up the foundations of many generations; and thou shalt be called, The repairer of the breach, The restorer of paths to dwell in."   — Isaiah 55:3; 58:9-12

"Even as a child, she seems to have troubled her parents, to whom being comfortable was an end of life, and who refused to or could not understand her mission. . . . At the age of five, she refused to eat sugar, as long as the soldiers at the front were not able to get it. The war brought the sense of human misery into her protected milieu for the first time, and her typical pattern of response was already set: to deny herself what the most unfortunate were unable to enjoy. . . . At fourteen, she passed through the darkest spiritual crisis of her life, feeling herself pushed to the very verge of suicide by an acute sense of her absolute unworthiness, and by the onslaught of migraine headaches of an unbearable intensity. The headaches never left her afterward, not even in her moments of extremest joy. . . . "I may say that never in my life have I 'sought for God'," she said toward the end of her life; but she had been all the time waiting, without daring to define what she awaited. . . . "In a moment of intense physical suffering," she tells us, "when I was forcing myself to feel love, but without desiring to give a name to that love, I felt, without being in any way prepared for it . . . a presence more personal, more certain, more real than that of a human being, though inaccessible to the senses and the imagination."   — Simone Weil (WG)

1 January 1969

"Dear Aunt Gail:

"A while ago, you asked about what my friend, Nancy, believed about miracles. Well, she felt, as I do, that they happen every single day — in the lives of people who believe — really believe in the presence of God in their everyday lives. She said that she could ask God for help with anything, anytime, and He would help (maybe not in the way she asked — or im-

103

mediately upon asking but God never failed her). These are her miracles — as well as mine.

"When I am frustrated, lost, tired, or in need of any help — if I ask God to please help me (and believe that everything will turn out fine because it is in His hands) then I receive help and as long as I truly remember to thank God — heartily — then He is always willing to help. I think the formula of life for me can be summed up like this —

"Have Faith, and let it happen!

All my love,

Chris"

"This is the *summum bonum*. . . ."

"This life is but one stage in the growth of the self. As the soul of man did not wholly originate out of nature or society so it cannot find complete fulfillment through nature or society. Man is called upon to adjust to the environment, to reality; but the total real environment includes the spiritual order as well as the natural and the social order, and so long as man has not made the supreme adjustment, his adjustment remains incomplete. Man's ultimate aim is to realize his union with God and/or the Absolute Reality. This is the *summum bonum;* it is the experience which dispels all doubts and dissipates all dissatisfaction; it brings consummate happiness and the peace that passeth understanding. At least a glimpse of it may be achieved in the present life through the mystical experience; alongside it, all the other satisfactions which life has to offer are temporary, and fragmentary; by means of it man is restored to wholeness and made free. Whether one speaks of salvation, liberation, enlightenment or the beatific vision, one tends to emphasize the fact that life is a training ground, in which man ought to be preparing himself for his last end — the achievement of super-consciousness. This is the aim of life, not the widest dispersal of creature comforts, or even the achievement of a social utopia, but the evocation of higher and intenser forms of consciousness. Life is a process of self-realization, of self-discovery and self-transformation."

— Bernard Phillips (SR)

Age 10 through 16

[James lives on the West Coast. He is the youngest of three brothers. We have known his mother and father since before they were married. In May 1962, when James was ten, his father died after a brief illness. A few weeks later, James and his mother and brothers came for a week-end visit. On one of the days, James and I went for a walk. We walked and walked, not saying anything. Finally, James said, "what shall we talk about?" I said, "what do you want to talk about?" "Nothing much," he said, so we didn't. We just walked through the lower pasture where the sheep were, stopping here and there to look out across the hills or examine some outcropping of rock that the earth had tossed up millions of years ago, or to pick a few Spring flowers that were beginning to bloom again. James and his family visit us often — always in the summers. James comes on school week-ends when there is something special he has thought of or read and wants to discuss. And often he leaves notes behind for me to read later; and we write when we have something to say. Here are some of the notes and letters from James.]

The camera is held by man.
The man's thoughts are inside
the camera. If man does not
apply the work of his thoughts
the picture, which represents
good will not come out. If
the good doesn't come out
than the evil will take
over. This point shows
man must be careful.

5. B. M. Mar, 23, 1962

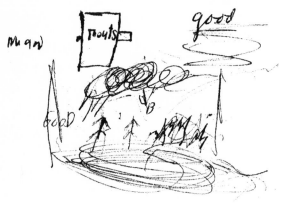

Man must find to use what he has.
If he has food he can do work. Work
to create or work to improve himself

7:30 P.M   Nov. 23 1962
on finding this in The Divine Milieu.

O, god help this child
to become
what I wanna is
in him —
23 Dec. 62

Dear Gail;

   While I was doing my homework I paused for a moment and an idea came into my head
which was that a milk carton represented a boys goal and that a boy must want to
drink it if he should want to be a man. HE was already given milk to form his bones
but wether or not he wants to continue it is up to him.
        This shows that every one is given the seed but wether or not he or she are
interested in it is whether they want to grow up.

                Love,

                James

P. S. Tpse books I talked about did not have any thing on our subject.

"Whom shall He teach knowledge? and whom shall He make to understand 'the hearing'? them that are weaned from the milk, and are drawn from the breasts. For precept hath been upon precept, precept upon precept; line upon line, line upon line; here a little, and there a little."

— Isaiah 28:9-10

"Wherefore laying aside all malice, and all guile, and hypocrisies, and envies, and all evil speakings, As newborn babes, desire the sincere milk of the word, that ye may grow thereby: If so be ye have tasted that the Lord *is* gracious, Ye also, as lively stones built up a spiritual house . . . a chosen generation . . . that ye should show forth the praises of Him who hath called you out of the darkness into his marvellous light. . . ."

— 1 Peter 2:1-9

Feb. 13, 1963

"Dear Gail,

"I thought I would write you because one of the biggest things I have conceived so far in our *Cosmic Consciousness** came about last night. This morning I had it in a way which I couldn't describe to you in words.

"Well, it all started out last night about 9:30 P.M. When I got into bed I was sort of thinking about this subject when a sudden thought entered my mind which was: How could I communicate with God? I stopped there and then chuckled in my mind and went to sleep.

"My last dream which I suppose started at 6:15 A.M. (I got up at 6:45) but how it struck my mind I do not recall. My father, however, did appear. I was so very glad to see him that I cried in my dream for joy. We went everywhere I could think of. When I was beginning to wake up he told me that he did not die and that he had just changed forms (I really mean this)

108

forms like you believed. He also said that he would go with me *wherever* I went even though I couldn't feel, touch, see him.

"I got up and as this burst of energy — it was the highest I have ever had it. It still is with me. I don't really know whether it is my reaction to this thing or $e = E^2$. It stunned me all through the day.

"This peculiarity solved another answer of mine. Could I ever communicate with my father again, and I did through God, and a dream. I forgot to mention one other thing that my mother said to me: my father was a brilliant man. I had only known my father to be my father instead of a man of medicine. I know so much more in the human body than last May, I only wish I could have known him then as I do now I thought. Then, too, we brought a model of the brain to school of my father's model he made in medical school. It was so complex I knew he must have been a great man to make it for Cornell kept the model for 16 years after he left there because it was so very good. I didn't exactly know how to tell the class but they understood for themselves how complex it was. So this is my way of still communicating with my father even though he is not alive on the earth today, by dreams. I could go on and on about this but I feel I have covered it pretty well. One other thing though before I drop this is that not only by dreams but by Cosmic Consciousness, for without it I could not interpret any of the messages whatsoever.

"Speaking of the day I was sick last week, I suddenly got this good feeling. I, even though sick, got a good feeling which lasted twelve minutes. I cleaned my room to a whistle. It is not that I don't have time to get tired, but it is not thought of, you just can't think of getting tired.

"This has probably been my biggest day since May 19, 1962**
"Have a ball on Valentine and don't forget

$$e = E^2{***}$$

Love,
James"

"P. S. I can use some of my birthday money to come up to your place to tell you the whole story (I got parts written down.) Maybe on Washington's Birthday — I get out Thursday the 21st at noon and go back Monday. Please write."

[Note: *Cosmic consciousness — These words, and why James used them, are explained on the following pages. **May 19th, 1962, was the day James' father died. ***e $= E^2$ (with James' signature) is a 'formula' we made up:

> e is for effort
> your effort and mine
> E^2 is a Gift
> when we try.

This applies to work or study or trying to know more about God and His will. If we put forth our effort, we are given added strength, or knowledge or wisdom.]

Cosmic Consciousness

"Only a personal experience of it . . . will enable us to realize what this actually is. . . ."   — Dr. R. M. Bucke (CC)

"What is Cosmic Consciousness? The present volume is an attempt to answer this question; but notwithstanding it seems well to make a short prefatory statement in as plain language as possible so as to open the door, as it were, for the more elaborate exposition to be attempted in the body of the work. Cosmic Consciousness, then, is a higher form of consciousness than that possessed by the ordinary man. . . . The prime characteristic of cosmic consciousness is, as the name implies, a consciousness of the cosmos, that is, of the life and order of the universe. What these words mean cannot be touched upon here; it is the business of this volume to throw some light upon them. There are many elements belonging to the cosmic sense besides the central fact just alluded to. Of these a few may be mentioned. Along with the consciousness of the cosmos there occurs an intellectual enlightenment or illumination which alone would place the individual on a new plane of existence — would make him almost a member of a new species. To this is added a state of moral exaltation, an indescribable feeling of elevation, elation and joyousness, and a quickening of the moral sense, which is fully as striking and more important both to the individual and to the race than is the enhanced intellectual power. With these come, what may be called, a sense of immortality, a consciousness of eternal life, not a conviction that he shall have this, but the consciousness that he has it already.

"Only a personal experience of it, or a prolonged study of men who have passed into this new life, will enable us to realize what this actually is. . . ."

— Dr. Richard Maurice Bucke (CC)

[Note: James used the words 'cosmic consciousness' because I had tried to explain what enabled him to have such wonderful thoughts.]

"This shows that every one is given the seed, but whether or not he or she is interested in it is whether they want to grow up."

— James, age 10

". . . Mankind is still in the making. Human life as we have it is only the raw material for human life as it might be. . . ."

— S. Radhakrishnan (ER)

". . . and it doth not yet appear what we shall be."

— 1 John 3:2

[The following is a Dedicatory Letter that Dr. Bucke wrote to his son, which appeared in a first Limited Edition of his book.]

111

MAURICE ANDREWS BUCKE
22 November 1868 — 8 December 1899

8 December 1900

"Dear Maurice:

"A year ago to-day, in the prime of youth, of health and of strength, in an instant, by a terrible and fatal accident, you were removed forever from this world in which your mother and I still live. Of all young men I have known you were the most pure, the most noble, the most honorable, the most tender-hearted. In the business of life you were industrious, honest, faithful, intelligent and entirely trustworthy. How at the time we felt your loss — how we still feel it — I would not set down even if I could. I desire to speak here of my confident hope, not of my pain. I will say that through the experiences which under-lie this volume I have been taught, that in spite of death and the grave, although you are beyond the range of our sight and hearing, notwithstanding that the universe of sense testifies to your absence, you are not dead and not really absent, but alive and well and not far from me this moment. If I have been permitted — no, not to enter, but — through the narrow aperture of a scarcely opened door, to glance one instant into that other divine world, it was surely that I might thereby be enabled to live through the receipt of those lightning-flashed words from Montana which time burns only deeper and deeper into my brain.

"Only a little while now we shall be again together and with us those other noble and well-beloved souls gone before. I am sure I shall meet you and them; that you and I shall talk of a thousand things and of that unforgettable day and of all that followed it; and that we shall clearly see that all were parts of an infinite plan which was wholly wise and good. Do you see and approve as I write these words? It may well be. Do you read from within what I am now thinking and feeling? If you do you know how dear to me you were while you yet lived what we call life here and how much more dear you have become to me since.

112

"Because of the indissoluble links of birth and death wrought by nature and fate between us; because of my love and because of my grief; above all because of the infinite and inextinguishable confidence there is in my heart, I inscribe to you this book, which, full as it is of imperfections which render it unworthy of your acceptance, has nevertheless sprung from the divine assurance born of the deepest insight of the noblest members of your race.

"So long! dear boy.

Your Father"

"The gift of real understanding is given to a few. The world is dependent upon them for the future. They are the missionaries of God. Love, James."
— [A Postcard from James
Sent from Europe — Summer, 1963]

"A gift is as a precious stone in the eyes of him that hath it." . . . "The stone which the builders refused is become the head stone of the corner. This is the Lord's doing; it is marvellous in your eyes." — Prov. 17:8; Psm. 118:22-23

"Ye are the salt of the earth . . . ye are the light of the world. ". . . the shining light that shineth more and more unto the perfect day." ". . . For it is God that worketh in you both to will and to do of His good pleasure. Do all things without murmurings and disputings: That ye may be blameless and sincere, the sons of God, without rebuke, in the midst of a crooked and perverse nation, among whom ye shine as lights in the world."
— Matt: 5:13-14; Proverbs 4:18; Phil. 2:13-14-15

Oct. 23, 1963

"Dear Gail,

"I wrote you mainly because what has happened in just a few days. I began setting aside a time of the day which I could put in for thinking.

113

"I started thinking about the difference between S. F. and A. S. F. has polluted air and other industrial things of a city which would greatly interfere with the atmosphere. Second, you have natural beauties, fields, river, garden which we don't have. Third, many interruptions are all over S. F.: loud radios, many people, buses, cars, etc. You have very few because you are in the country. 4. I think your place is perfect for this special atmosphere and much better than S. F.

"A few incidents such as in science have taken place. We were discussing that man could never be fully happy (on average basis, scientifically) because he always asks why. Then towards the end of the period one boy brought up that spiritual people are said to be happy all their lives. He then said that this is different and was beyond *our* mental intelligence. (So he thinks.) My mother said also, that she loved me very much for this faith that we have when she was depressed.

"Then what had really happened is what I'm going to tell you. I was down at the main branch library and I looked for a book on this subject. I looked in philosophy and found a marvelous book which you probably have heard of, *Founding the Life Divine* by Morwenna Donnelly and published by Hawthorn Books, Inc. N.Y. 1956. One of the quotations I got from it was:

'To see nothing but the Divine, to be at ever in union with him, to love him in all creatures and have the light of him in all things is the whole condition of his (the spiritual man's) existence. His God-vision does not divorce him from life, nor does he miss any of the fulness of life, for God, himself, becomes spontaneous to him. . . . The joy of heaven, of earth are only a small shadow of his possessions; for he grows into the Divine; the Divine, too, flows out of him with all the light, power and joy of an infinite experience.' (From Essays of the GITA.)

"From that I was so overjoyed because I understood it and that it was the most divine thing I have ever heard. At this point

I was so filled with *pure* love, truth and happiness, I came to the highest point of cosmic consciousness I ever have had. During the summer I had two blooms, as I told you, however, they were not as big as this one. Then my thoughts started rolling. I wanted to say something for what I thought my soul was really like and I suddenly got the thought that your soul (or flower) will open its petals (the bonds that tie us to mortal life) and if you let it, it will burst open to see the sun (God). Also other short thoughts like: Let God live in you, he will help your soul grow if you let him and others which I won't go into.

"Also, you were talking about a young child growing up with a pure soul since it was too young to know or to really have any thought of reality. I thought this had to be true because a child doesn't really know much. Also, if you can get a child about 6 or 7 thinking about this (cosmic consciousness) he will not lose it and could be much of a benefit. Finally, about my age, if a boy or girl doesn't know about this at any age they tend to forget about it and that's why you would usually tell a child about this between 5 — 13.

"Love of all kinds,

James

$e = E^2$"

[Note: At this time, James was 11 and both his question about what his soul 'was really like' and his answer were spontaneous and original. Four years later, during one of his visits I asked him again, and his answer is his letter dated Sept. 1, 1967.]

"Train up a child in the way he should go: and when he is old, he will not depart from it."   — Proverbs 22:6

"He that diligently seeketh good procureth favour: but he that seeketh mischief, it shall come unto him."
— Proverbs 11:27

"But he that received seed into the good ground is he that heareth the word, and understandeth it; which also beareth fruit, and bringeth forth, some hundredfold, some sixty, some thirty."   — Matt. 13:23

Jan. 3, 1964

"Dear Gail and Charles,

"I am so very sorry about Specky's death. I know how you loved him so very much as I do. But we have one thing to be glad about, he has gone to God's kingdom to live forever. That is the wonderful part that he, like every other living thing, is allowed to go through the gates of heaven. We have those good memories to cherish which we will have forever.

· "Gail, I have really been reading *The Spirit of Man* and I find it most extraordinary. A chapter on 'joy' and the respect of one's soul have been marvelous like many others. I have learned by giving real respect for one's soul you feel true happiness within you. Real 'Joy is possible only when we are driven towards things and persons because of *what they are* and *not* because of what we can get from them. . . .'Joy is nothing else than *awareness* of our being fulfilled in our *true being,* in our personal center. And this fulfillment is possible only if *we right ourselves with what we really are.'*

"The other book called *Uncle Tom's Cabin* by Harriet Beecher Stowe, is a book I'm sure you have heard about. It mostly is north and south attitudes staging to the civil war. But the other plot is about Uncle Tom and Miss Eva who finally die going to heaven having this gift. Tom was a martyr who died because of his faith. His master tried to make him disbelieve in God and finally was whipped to death. Miss Eva was a seven year old girl who read Uncle Tom the Bible at a previous estate. She one evening was reading the Bible to him and saw the gates of heaven and told everyone she was going there soon. You could hear what they thought and it was so wonderful I think you ought to read the book (I'll bring it to you.) Since I read the book I feel it really has taught me a lot. It has taught me

116

more about a stronger faith and love for God and for everyone. The other day I sprained my finger very badly in a basketball game. I went home on the bus and it hurt so very much and I couldn't do a thing. I prayed to God to stop the pain and in 10-15 minutes I felt no pain. There have been other wonderful experiences that would take too long on a letter to tell you. I love you both and Specky also.

James"

"P.S. Thank you so very much for the book. Will see you soon I hope."

[Note: *The Spirit of Man* is an anthology edited by Whit Burnett (Hawthorn Books, Inc. 1958). The lines James quoted, with his own underscoring, are from the chapter by Paul Tillich, pages 260 and 261. When James speaks of Uncle Tom and Miss Eva "having this gift," he is referring to a higher consciousness — mentioned in his letter of February 13, 1963.]

["Day Before Easter — 2:30 To Gail — While having an ebb and flow today while reading 'The Cloud Unknowing' *divine* I thought of all I read and I find in conclusion that God reveals everything through love, and through Love everything may reveal itself to God." (James left this note after one of his visits. He had been in the library reading "The Cloud of Unknowing" A fourteenth-century devotional classic by an unknown author; Harper & Brothers, 1948.)]

"It is written in the prophets, And they shall be taught of God."
". . . Of His own will begat He us with the word of truth."
". . . ye yourselves are taught of God to love one another."
". . . By this shall all men know that ye are my disciples, if ye have love one for another."

— John 6:45; James 1:18;
1 Thess. 4:9; John 13:35

"Tagore's mysticism was nothing but his sense of kinship with everything, his innate awareness of the unseen link that binds all the living together as well as the living with the so-called nonliving, the seen with the unseen. In that sense this mystic awareness was deep-rooted in his soul from his childhood. It had always stirred within him. Its 'sprouting' at this period of his life in his poetry simply means that his search for this link in his own life, his quest for the guiding Muse of his genius and destiny, the Personality within and above his personality, became more conscious. In a letter dated 24 March 1894, he wrote: 'I am overwhelmed by this awareness of the baffling mystery within me which I can neither understand nor control. I know not where it will take me or I it, I know not what I can do or cannot do. I cannot see, nor am I consulted about, what surges up in my heart, what flows in my veins, what stirs in my brain, and yet I move about and keep up the pretence that I am the master of my thoughts and deeds. I am like a living pianoforte with a complicated network of wires hidden within it, but what makes it play and who comes suddenly to play on it and when and why, I do not know. . . .' " — Krishna Kripalani (T)

April 20, 1967

"Dear Gail,

"Thank you so very much for the book on Radhakrishnan — I think it is an excellent book that has a lot to say, and Gandhi's passage on war and its outcome. What you say about understanding things later on I find very true. In just a few short years I find new meaning and insight in what I read.

"Also picked up a book on The Medium Is The Message. John had recommended it. McLuhan's views primarily concern the idea man is regressing the world to a single tribal village through mass media. He really has something shocking to say.

"Perhaps if we get some better weather, I'd love to visit you some weekend. There is a lot to talk over. Again many thanks,

"Love,

James"

"My soul has grown deep like the rivers."

— Langston Hughes (DA)

"And I gave my heart to seek and search out by wisdom concerning all things that are done under the heaven: this sore travail hath God given to the sons of man to be exercised therewith." . . . Happy is the man that findeth wisdom, and the man that getteth understanding . . . better than . . . silver . . . and the gain thereof than fine gold . . . and all the things thou canst desire are not to be compared unto her. Length of days is in her right hand; and in her left hand riches and honour. Her ways are the ways of pleasantness, and all her paths are peace. She is the tree of life to them that lay hold upon her: and happy is *every one* that retaineth her."

— Eccl. 1:13; Prov. 3:13-18

119

Sept 1
'67

Dear Gail + Charles

I can't thank you enough for
letting me spend a few days. It was really
enjoyable and most pleasurable.

Gail, I hesitated a while in writing
this letter so I could take time and answer
your question carefully. I found the answer
while I was camping with a friend in upper
Yosemite I realized my soul is but a small
stream It appeared to me that it was quite
young, that it had a glimpse of where it
was going but had such a long way to go.
I envisioned the many rapids I must pass
over, the many valleys I had to go through

120

on my way to the giver of all life (in
this case, the sea). I saw that as I grew
I would be taken in by the mightier rivers
and by the same power that made me a stream,
I would become part of a still greater stream.
(I suppose it might be a metaphor to reincarnation)
Then also I thought about those times when
during the course of my rapid flow I would
stop and become a pool of water, stopping to
reflect the life around me. It would be like
a moment to rest and to see things as they
really are. And then only too soon, would I
be caught up in my only little ways and
pursue the path from which I had temporarily
broken off.
                    Well, I guess that gives you an

idea of what my soul really looks like. It requires great concentration to get a glimpse of ones soul. It seems as though you must get completely out of yourself then take a look at what you've removed yourself from. A most wonderful thing though —

Again many thanks for everything

Love
James

"Neither can they die any more: for they are equal unto the angels; and are the children of God, being the children of the resurrection." . . . "Behold, what manner of love the Father hath bestowed upon us, that we should be called the sons of God . . . and it doth not yet appear what we shall be."
— Luke 20:36; 1 John 3:1-2

[Note: James left these notes after one of his weekend visits.]

Aug 25, '67

"The whole universe is
a fast struggle to realize
the unity which is the ideal
The tension of the universe is
mirrored in man, reflected
in his individuality

"the self separates itself
from itself to return to
itself to be itself"

You feel love you know love
Love is you...

VII

"I THINK A SOUL IS LIFE AND TRUTH. . . ."

Cheryl
10

I think a soul is life and truth. Without it we would not exist. It is a part of our conscience because if you dis-obey, it hurts. Your soul is at every part of your body at every time. It is a spirit, telling you what to do. I don't belive anyone could live without it. It is in-ner thoughts reflected from your personial life.

125

"At that moment I experienced the presence of the Divine as I had never before experienced him. It seemed as though I could hear the quiet assurance of an inner voice, saying, 'Stand up for righteousness, stand up for truth. God will be at your side forever.' Almost at once my fears began to pass from me. My uncertainty disappeared. I was ready to face anything. The outer situation remained the same, but God had given me inner calm."   — Martin Luther King, Jr. (SL)

"I am no authority on Metaphysics. In any controversial discussion regarding monism and dualism I shall remain silent. I only say from what I feel that my innermost God has a joy in expressing Himself through me — This joy, this love pervades every part of my being, suffusing my mind, my intellect, this entire universe which is so vivid before me, my infinite past and my eternal destiny. . . . In it are reflected all life's joys and sorrows, all shades of light and darkness.

"All this that is being moulded within me, and He who is moulding it — between both there is a joyous relationship, there is a bond of perpetual love. When I am convinced of this, a peace steals over me through all circumstances, through joy as well as sorrow. When I realize that every outburst of mine uttered in joy, that every sorrow and pain I have suffered from, He has drawn close to Him, accepting it as His own, I know then that nothing has been a waste or in vain — everything has been blessed towards a completeness overspreading the universe. . . .

"Whatever I build up to perfection with my life-efforts is the ultimate truth for me. When we experience the joys and sorrows of our lives as separate and as final, we cannot comprehend the mystery of this eternal creation that takes place within us. . . . But, when once the unity of a continuous thread in the creative faculty within us is grasped, we come to realize that we have some affinity with this infinite universe including all its moving and motionless created beings. I know that just as the stars, the planets, the sun and the moon shall ever exist in Creation, through constant burning, through ever revolving, so there has been in me a constant creative process from time immemorial

— my happiness and my suffering, my aches and desires thus fall into place. What will be the outcome of all this I do not know; even the smallest particle of dust is not quite known to us. Standing away from myself, when I look at my over-flowing life uniting it with the eternity of time and space, I see then that even my sorrows have been grafted into one massive joy. I exist, I am becoming, I am moving — this I know to be a miraculous happening. I exist — and along with me everything else exists. Beyond me not even an atom or a molecule of this illimitable world can exist."

— Rabindranath Tagore (TT)

"Unlike many modern thinkers, he (Tagore) had no blueprint for the world's salvation. He believed in no 'isms'. He merely emphasized certain basic truths which men of wisdom have known in all ages and which men may ignore only at their peril. His thought will therefore never be out of date. . . . However we (the East and the West) may seem to differ, we come of the same earth, are moulded of the same clay — the shade may vary somewhat — and are lit by the same spark which we call divine because it is beyond our manipulation and our comprehension. We grow by giving and taking and our destinies are intertwined. If this is not true, then all religions are a mockery and all our science a snare made by man for his self-destruction. This is the essence of Tagore's message, as it is the essence of all philosophy and wisdom, eastern or western. . . .
"In their utterance we feel the glow of a heightened moral consciousness which one gets in the contemporary writings of such American idealists as Thoreau, Emerson and Walt Whitman."

— Krishna Kripalani (T)

"Throughout the centuries men have sought to discover the highest good. . . . What is the *summum bonum* of life? I think I have found the answer, America. I have discovered that the highest good is love. This is the principle at the center of the cosmos. It is the greatest unifying force of life. God is love. He who loves has discovered the clue to the meaning of ultimate reality." — Martin Luther King, Jr. (SL)

"The binding principle which sustains the universe is co-operation. In theological terms it is put down as 'love'."
> — S. Radhakrishnan
> (Letter — March 14, 1967)

"The Creation is an act of love, and it is something that is going on perpetually. At every moment our existence is God's love for us."   — Simone Weil (N)

"The Lord hath appeared from afar unto me, saying, Yea, I have loved thee with an everlasting love: therefore with loving-kindness have I drawn thee."   — Jeremiah 31:3

"I subscribe to the belief or the philosophy that all life in its essence is one, and that the humans are working consciously or unconsciously towards the realization of that identity. This belief requires a living faith in a living God who is the ultimate arbiter of our fate. Without Him not a blade of grass moves."
> — Gandhi (SG)

"There is nothing on earth that I would not give up for the sake of the country excepting, of course, two things and two only, namely, truth and non-violence. I would not sacrifice these two for all the world. For, to me, Truth is God and there is no way to find Truth except the way of non-violence. I do not seek to serve India at the sacrifice of Truth or God. For I know that a man who forsakes Truth can forsake his country, and his nearest and dearest ones."
> — Gandhi (*India News,* 13 Sept. 1968)

". . . unarmed love is the most powerful force in the world."
> — Martin Luther King, Jr. (SL)

"It is unnecessary to believe in an extra mundane Power called God in order to sustain our faith in *ahimsa*. But God is not a Power residing in the clouds. God is an unseen Power residing within us and nearer to us than finger-nails to the flesh. There are many powers lying hidden within us and we discover them by constant struggle. Even so may we find this Supreme Power if we make diligent search with the fixed determination to find Him. One such way is the way of *ahimsa*. It is so very necessary because God is in every one of us, and, therefore, we have to identify ourselves with every human being without exception. This is called cohesion or attraction in scientific language. In the popular language it is called love. It binds us to one another and to God. *Ahimsa* and love are one and the same thing. I hope this is all clear to you."   — Gandhi (SG)

"And he lifted up his eyes on his disciples, and said, Blessed be ye poor: for yours is the kingdom of God. Blessed are ye that hunger now: for ye shall be filled. Blessed are ye that weep now: for ye shall laugh. Blessed are ye, when men shall hate you, and when they shall separate you *from their company,* and shall reproach you, and cast out your name as evil. . . . Rejoice ye in that day, and leap for joy, for, behold, your reward is great in heaven. . . . I say unto you which hear, Love your enemies, do good to them that hate you, Bless them that curse you, and pray for them which despitefully use you. And unto him that smiteth thee on one cheek offer also the other. . . . And as ye would that men should do to you, do ye also to them likewise. For if ye love them which love you, what thank have ye? for sinners also love those that love them. And if ye do good to them which do good to you, what thank have ye? the sinners also do even the same. . . . But love ye your enemies, and do good, and lend, hoping for nothing again; and your reward shall be great, and ye shall be the children of the Highest: for he is kind unto the unthankful and to the evil."
                    — Luke 6: 20-23; 27-29; 31-33 and 35
                        *   *   *

"What does your soul look like?
It does not look like a human being but yet it has the feature.
It does not have ears but it has the ability to receive and deceive.
It is stronger than a physical body, it is a spiritual being.
The soul is the highest degree of being — even after death it has the ability to live on.

It is acquainted with many objects of which it has been associated with.

It looks like eternal life — it has no shape or size.

It is larger than anything, yet man cannot see it.

It is like the wind — no one can know where it came from nor where it is going but it is there — so is the soul.

This is what I really think."   — Denise, age 16

"What does your soul look like? It looks like happiness. Love or peace."   — Larry, age 10

"What does your soul look like? People have bad souls and good souls. A soul is a conscience. You have bad consciences and good consciences. Everybody has a conscience and everybody has a soul, but some people don't believe it. One conscience tells you good as your good conscience does, and bad conscience tells you a bad thing to do."   — David, age 9

"What does your soul look like? It looks like God."

                                        — David, age 10

"My soul looks like a circle with a fire burning in the middle and stars surrounding it."   — Hartman, age 10

"It is my religion. My inside: it tells me what to do. It is invisible. You cannot see it but I can feel it."

                                        — Joel, age 11

"My soul looks like a long low sigh, that is what I think it looks like."   — Carol, age 10

*   *   *

"For we know that the whole creation — every creature — groaneth and travaileth in pain together until now. And not only they, but ourselves, also, which have the firstfruits of the Spirit, even we ourselves groan within ourselves. . . ." "But if we hope for that we see not, *then* we do with patience wait for *it*.

"Likewise the Spirit also helpeth our infirmities: for we know not what we should pray for as we ought; but the Spirit itself maketh intercession for us with groanings which cannot be uttered." . . . "And we know that all things work together for good to them that love God, to them who are called according to his purpose." — Romans 8:22-23, 25-26, 28

"My soul looks like a ghost that is small but friendly and has influence on others. It wants me to help the problems in the world but since it is small it thinks it cannot do anything to help." — Jeff, age 11

"The son shall not bear the iniquity of the father, neither shall the father bear the iniquity of the son." . . . "Repent and turn *yourselves* from all your transgressions . . . and make you a new heart and a new spirit." — Ezekiel 18:20, 30 and 31

"By our self-improvement we improve the world." — S. Radhakrishnan (Letter, 1962)

"Self-discovery, self-knowledge . . . is man's destiny.
"When we enter the world of ideals the differences among religions become negligible and the agreements striking. There is only one ideal for man, to make himself profoundly human, perfectly human. 'Be ye perfect.' The whole man, the complete man, is the ideal man, the divine man. 'You are complete in the godhead', said St. Paul. The seeking for our highest and in-most self is the seeking for God. Self-discovery, self-knowledge, self-fulfilment is man's destiny." — S. Radhakrishnan (ER)

"Mankind is still in the making.
"In spite of all appearances to the contrary, we discern in the present unrest the gradual dawning of a great light, a converging life-endeavor, a growing realization that there is a secret spirit in which we are all one, and of which humanity is the highest vehicle on earth, and an increasing desire to live out this knowl-edge and establish a kingdom of spirit on earth. Science has

131

produced the necessary means for easy transport of men and communication of thought. Intellectually the world is bound together in a web of common ideas and reciprocal knowledge. Even the obstacles of religious dogma are not so formidable as they were in the past. The progress of thought and criticism is helping the different religions to sound the note of the eternal, the universal, the one truth of spirit which life obeys, seeks for, and delights in at all times and in all places. We are able to see a little more clearly that the truth of a religion is not what is

What does your soul look like?

Karyn Age 10½

I think the way you yourself can see your soul is the way other people see your true self and your own personality.
Your soul is the way you act to others. Your soul is the way you feel about others.
What is soul?

There are many answers to this question.
I think that soul comes from the heart.
You have to believe and understand yourself to say WHY you act this certain way.
Soul is the way you believe in God.
What does your soul look like?
Soul is love + hate; the difference between life & death.

Do you think you have a good soul?

132

singular and private to it, is not the mere letter of the law which its priests are apt to insist on, and its faithful to fight for, but that part of which it is capable of sharing with all others. Humanity's ultimate realization of itself and of the world can be attained only by an ever-increasing liberation of the values that are universal and human. Mankind is still in the making. Human life as we have it is only the raw material for human life as it might be. There is a hitherto undreamt-of fullness, freedom, and happiness within reach of our species, if only we can pull ourselves together and go forward with a high purpose and fine resolve. What we require is not professions and programmes but the power of the spirit in the hearts of men, a power which will help us to discipline our passions of greed and selfishness and organize the world which is at one with us in desire. . . . There is a region beyond the body and the intellect, one in which the human spirit finds its expression in aspiration, not in formulas, a region which Plato enters when he frames his myths. It is called the soul of a being, the determining principle of body and mind. In the souls of men to-day there are clashing tides of colour and race, nation and religion, which create mutual antagonisms, myths, and dreams that divide mankind into hostile groups. Conflicts in human affairs are due to divisions in the human soul. . . . The one doctrine that has the longest intellectual ancestry is the belief that the ordinary condition of man is not his ultimate being, that he has in him a deeper self, call it breath or ghost, soul or spirit. In each being dwells a light which no power can extinguish, an immortal spirit, benign and tolerant, the silent witness of his heart. The greatest thinkers of the world unite in asking us to know the self. Mencius declares: 'Who knows his own nature knows heaven.' St. Augustine writes: 'I, Lord, went wandering like a strayed sheep, seeking thee with anxious reasoning without, whilst thou wast within me. . . . I went round the streets and squares of the city of this world seeking thee, and I found thee not, because in vain I sought without for him who was within myself.' We make a detour round the universe to get back to the self. The oldest wisdom in the world tells us that we can consciously unite with the divine while in this body, for this is man really born. If he misses his destiny, Nature is not in a hurry; she will catch him some day and compel him to fulfil her secret purpose. Truth, beauty, peace, power, and wisdom are all attributes of the divine self which awaits our finding."   — S. Radhakrishnan (ER)

[In accepting the fellowship of Sahitya Akademi (India's Academy of Letters), Dr. S. Radhakrishnan, former Ambassador to the Soviet Union, former President of India, and world-renowned philosopher, said:]

" 'It is essential for us to recognize that the greatness of man consists not in the knowledge he acquires or the power he possesses, but in the spirit of pure, unselfish and disinterested love of the world. It is that wisdom that we have to cultivate.'

"Dr. Radhakrishnan exhorted the members of the Akademi to recognize the primary importance of the spiritual direction of life and to try to make contributions which would 'enable us to elevate our spirit'. He said, 'We have today neglected spiritual values with the result that nations which have achieved great knowledge and great power are suspected to be bringing the world to the brink of disaster.'

"Dr. Radhakrishnan said articulation was the most precious possession of man, and literature was the highest expression of articulation. Literature was of different kinds — knowledge, power, spirit. Knowledge and power were instruments and spirit must give the direction, he said. But wisdom of the heart was more important than any other kind of wisdom.

" 'We have to cultivate that wisdom because it transcends all boundaries of race, nation, religion and ideology.' He also wanted the people to cultivate a commitment to world understanding and to social responsibilities of bringing about peace."
          — (*India News*, 20 September 1968)

"Jesus saith unto them, Did ye never read in the scriptures, The stone which the builders rejected, the same is become the head of the corner: this is the Lord's doing, and it is marvellous in our eyes? Therefore say I unto you, The kingdom of God shall be taken from you, and given to a nation bringing forth the fruits thereof. And whosoever shall fall on this stone shall be broken: but on whomsoever it shall fall, it will grind him to powder.

"And when the chief priests and Pharisees heard his parables, they perceived that he spake of them. But when they sought to lay hands on him, they feared the multitude, because they took him for a prophet." — Matt. 21:41-46

"Get wisdom, get understanding: forget it not; . . . Forsake her not, and she shall preserve thee: love her and she shall keep thee. Wisdom is the principal thing; therefore get wisdom: and with all thy getting get understanding."
— Proverbs 4:5-6-7

"What avail, O builders of the world,
        unless ye build a safety for the soul."
        — Edwin Markham (DA)

"It is open to anyone to say that human nature has not been known to rise to such height. But if we have made unexpected progress in physical sciences, why may we do less in the science of the soul?" — Gandhi (SG)

Matt 12

1. My soul is Love, Peace, Freedom.
  It wants Love, peace, and Freedom.

135

"And a little child shall lead them. . . ."

— Isaiah 11:6

"And he shall turn the heart of the fathers to the children, and the heart of the children to their fathers. . . ."

— Malachi 4:6

My Soul looks like a tiny bit of the whole universe.

Cy   Age 12